GREEK MONASTIC ARCHITECTURE
an organic proposal

GREEK MONASTIC ARCHITECTURE
an organic proposal

Claudio Conenna

Primera edición   2007

Queda prohibida la reproducción total o parcial de esta obra incluido el diseño tipográfico y de portada sea cual fuere el medio, electrónico o mecánico, sin el consentimiento por escrito del editor.

©ARCHITECTHUM PLUS S.C.
Díaz de León 122-2 Aguascalientes, Aguascalientes,
México CP 20000

ISBN 978-968-9470-01-4

Prologue

The monastery, a Word coming from the Greek *Monastirio*, *monos* or alone and the suffix *–tirio* for where something takes place, namely a place to be alone[1], is not only a building that covers the practical necessities of cenobite monastic life. It is a building with an architectural character that solves other issues in its composition besides the necessarily functional and constructively technical ones for its preservation. It possesses a spatial structure and an enigmatic formal response that give a clear identity to the mystical aspect of monasticism. Metaphorically, we could say that it responds to the essence of Christian theology, expressed both in the Holy Scriptures and in the sayings and writings of the Eastern Holy Fathers. These texts, ever since the Early Christian era and in a continuous course until the post-Byzantine age, and a somehow weaker one until our time, are translated poetically into all the work of Eastern Christian Byzantine art, whether it is painting,, sculpture, music, literature, or architecture.

We should not forget that in the Byzantine age, Christian spirituality possessed a preponderant role in people's private and public daily life. During this period, Christian monasticism in the East, and especially in Greek territory, experienced an important growth. As a consequence of this, a number of cenobite monasteries was built. The most noteworthy examples of bulwarks of monasticism and monastery architecture are those of Mount Athos from the 10th century and later, those of Meteora in the 14th century, already in the post-Byzantine age. In these monastery complexes, we notice remarkable lessons of architecture that provide solutions with delicacy, from the criteria

---

[1] It should be clarified that the word *"alone"* does not include only the condition of the single man, but also the one implicitly container by the choice to live in this way, in cenobite solitude for *incessant prayer* with respect to worldly life in the family or other institutions. Besides, we can point out cases of monks who are widowers and others that decided to separate from their wives by mutual agreement in order for each of them to follow monastic life.

for location and the development of typologies to those of spatial organization and morphological expressions.

The monastery, as a spiritual institution, hosts a specific way of life: monasticism. There, the monk struggles for his own perfection and that of all humanity, since mankind and all creation have lost their main natural sense and are in a situation contrary to nature due to the "*fall*" or sin. The goal of the monk, in some way, is to succeed in regaining the lost ground and to reach the "*light*" and the "*truth*" again, graces that will dominate "*life*" with the arrival of the Kingdom of God[2]. Monks separate themselves from matters of the World, not out of enmity for it, but out of the desire to fully live God's will and reach "*His Image and Likeness*"[3]. Thus, poverty, chastity, and obedience are not simply three virtues that the monk struggles to obtain but rather three conditions for a spirituality that yearns for the eschatological perfection of human nature.

The path that he takes to reach it is the "*way*" of quietist (*Hesychast*) prayer[4], namely the understanding of "*introspection within oneself*" in silence[5], a vital protagonist in the monastery for monastic life, in which the monk humbly aspires to *Theopty*, or the vision of the Divine Light, and to *Theosis*, or the deification of human nature[6]. Consequently, the asceticism of the

---

[2] «....*Our salvation is now closer than when we began to have faith: night proceeds; day is near. Let us leave our own work of darkness and take up the weapons of light*...» Rom 13,12.

[3] Gen 1:26-27, 5:1, 9:6.

[4] From the Greek Ησυχία, transliterated Hesychia = calm, tranquility, silence, rest.

[5] Meyendorff J., *St. Gregory Palamas*, p. 138. On the spiritual character of silence, see Mt 6, 1-8, Ef. 1, 11-19. The sayings of the monks about the value of silence are equally characteristic: "...*Whoever learned to keep silence always finds rest... if you acquire the virtue of silence, do not boast that you gained something important. Convince yourself that you are not even worthy to speak...*", The Abbot Poemin, T. Hambaki, *Gerontikó*, p. 239-240.

[6] Concerning the spiritual concept of the Light, see in the New Testament Mt 5,13-16, Mt 6:22-24, Jn 1:8-9, Jn 8:12. In the

monks in Christ, although it is a strictly personal matter, taking a natural path through liturgical and cenobite life, maintains a clear ecclesiastical character. The monk does not only aspire to his own personal sanctification, but is also responsible for the final petition to the Creator by his universe[7].

In order for these matters to obtain an authentic theological meaning, concerning architecture we could affirm that monasteries express these perceptions in order to help the monk create the atmosphere that he needs in order to achieve complete communication with God and not exclusively to build spaces that cover practical needs *per se*. In this climate of silence and devotion, far away from the noise of the outside world, the monk attempts to silence internal noise with *introspection, self-denial, mysticism*, and *interiority*, in order to become imbued with the Divine Presence. These terms are translated architecturally in order for the monastery to take shape. In effect, in both the material aspect of the monastery and the theological one of monastic life, *humility* can be noticed in its overall volumetry, *simplicity* in its formal and technical solutions, and *sincerity* in the expression of the materials used. Humility that does not mean poverty and simplicity that does not acquire a simple-minded character.

From this point of view we can notice how the hypotheses and the base for the understanding of the creation of a monastery result from the development of Christian cenobite monasticism. The thought of its material creation begins, firstly, with the creation of a building program, a consequence of its program for life, which serves the practical and spiritual needs of the monks; secondly, with the selection of the site for the monastery complex; and thirdly, with the spatial organization and the

---

spirituality of Orthodox monasticism the Light was always fundamentally important: "*...When the prayer of Jesus becomes a prayer of the heart, the first result is enlightenment...*", see Serr J., *Filokalia*, p. 15.

[7] Zizioula, I, *La Creación,* p. 118-9.

placement of the basic elements of the program for the good functioning of the monastery as a building.

The predominant argument for the solution of a monastery program is the creation, in accordance with such a *way of life*, of a *place* or a *site* for a life of prayer, and the availability within it of the basic elements for the functional existence of the monastery as a community of cenobites[8]. The needs in terms of the program are the following: the *Katholikó* = the main church of the monastery, the refectory, the cells, and the supporting and service functions for the above such as the kitchen, warehouses, guest accommodation, and a stable. Nonetheless, in a noteworthy amount of monasteries, especially those located on Mount Athos, we find other program elements such as secondary chapels, the *phiale*, the defense tower and the bell tower, which reinforce the thematic identity of the medieval Byzantine monastery.

The monastery as an architectural fact is a building that covers the spiritual concerns of the monks. The *katholikó* is the spiritual refuge of the monks from *"evil"* and the defense tower is the corporal refuge protecting from the invasions that befell these holy places.

In Greece, the three *"columns"* of monastic form which are related to nature and define the mode of monastic asceticism are the following:

- **Agion Oros (Mount Athos) in Halkidiki,** of purely coenobitic form
- **Meteora in Thessaly,** coenobitic with leanings toward asceticism,
- **Gortynia in the Peloponnese,** a coenobitic settlement with an ascetic form, or an ascetic community.

Of course there are also other monastic complexes spread all over Greece which acquire or develop one of these forms of monastery, according to the monastic (coenobitic) leanings of the

---

[8] Cenobites, from the Greek *koinó* and *víos*, are those that live in common.

group of monks which identifies itself, following spiritual exercise, with the characteristics of the natural environment.[9] In general, most of the monasteries of Greece keep this regular monastic (coenobitic) form. The type of Meteora, however, is an exception within Greece and in the world of monastic architecture, since its topography is unique, in the shape of a giant "stone forest", where coenobitic monasteries leaning toward asceticism are set at the top of the rocks, in *"stylite"* fashion.

We could state in figurative terms that the symbolic system of architectural resolution of the monastery expresses the spirituality of monastic life, since a mimesis in dialogue between the real and the phenomenal is noted: the monastic and that of the monastery, the spiritual and the material, the devotional and the artistic, the mystical and the spatial, the experienced and the constructed.

Since the first step, namely the exact choice of the site, the monastery seems to bear implicitly within it the humble, serene, and risky duty of obeying the will of God. In more than a few cases, the sites chosen for the building of a monastery are truly inaccessible for apparent human capacity. If we take into account the era in which they were built, notwithstanding current high technology, we find ourselves with almost unsolvable difficulties in order to build on those sites. Although it is difficult to explain in scientific terms, we dare to think that desire, internal strength, and human self-sacrifice as an inclination towards solitude and spirituality, added to the divine call to or *"vocation"* for the life of prayer, are united and materialize at one point, in one place,

---

[9] Thus, there are monasteries with the same form as Gortynia of the Peloponnese, such as the Hozoviotissa monastery in Amorgos, the Zoodohos Piyi Kipina monastery in Epirus, the moanstery of Mega Spilaio at Kalavryta, and Eloni monastery at Leonidio. We also find groups with the same form as monasteries of Mount Athos in the community of Mystras, as well as the monastery of Saint John the Baptist in Serres, the monastery of Saint Vissarion in Trikala, and the monasteries of Osios Loukas and Osios Meletios in Central Greece, etc.

where the *monastic place* is built. This seems to be the result of mutual cooperation, of continuous dialogue between God and man or the response to a petition that is affirmed and confirmed in the daily vespers prayer with which the monk prays in expressed community with the Lord:

> «...*Show me the way that I must take, for I lift my soul to you. Teach me to fulfill your will, since you are my God...*» Psalm 142: 9-10.

Monastery Ag. Pavlos - Agion Oros

Based on these thoughts, a reasonable question could well be why monasteries are built in the *"desert"*, a preferred space for the construction of the majority of them. One reason to build them far from populated centers with an introverted spatial and volumetric expression would be based on considering monasticism as built on the two essential teachings of Christ: *self-denial*[10] and *prayer in secret*[11]. Thus, like Christ exhorts the Christian to pray in secret, isolated and separated from outside noise in order to extinguish internal noise, the monk retires to his cell, the cenobite community encloses itself in the monastery, and even a group of cenobite communities uproot themselves in the desert.

Another reason is found in the fact that the desert is the space where the echo of God's power resonates. Here, man comes in contact with nothingness, experiences it within himself, notices and feels his own weaknesses. At the same time, the soft, delicate, and subtle voice of the Savior is heard more clearly, a communication that facilitates a greater heightening and deepening of spiritual life. The soul is emptied of its desire for the external in order to allow internal fulfillment with divine presence.

This idea is reaffirmed in the typological organization, which is almost homogeneous in most cases. We are referring to the closed concentric type with the *katholikón* (the main church) at the center of the monastery, which would seem to fill it with its grandiose presence, if we look at it from a design perspective

---

[10] *«...If the grain of wheat does not fall on the ground and does not die, it remains alone, but if it dies, it bears much fruit. The one who loves his life destroys it, and the one who disdains his life in this world keeps it for eternal life. The one wishes to serve me, let him follow me and wherever I am, the one who serves me will be there. If someone serves me, my Father will honor him...»* Jn 12:24-26.

[11] *«...When you pray, go into your room, close the door, and pray to your Father who is in secret, and your Father who sees in secret will reward you...»* Mt 6, 6-7.

contrary to the real one[12], the empty space of the monastery's patio, where, in addition, the wings of the monastery embrace it, opening towards it by means of galleries. Besides, this representative system implicitly bears the idea that the monk should have as the *center* of his Christian monastic life the constant memory and vision of the Savior, of the life, death, and resurrection of the Divine Man, and in particular, in the condition of a monk, who *chose and was chosen, that is, called* to dedicate all his life to Christ completely.

All in all, the typological response does not leave aside respect for nature at any moment during the placement of a monastery. For this reason, other types of monastery architecture exist[13], the product in some cases of sacrifice of the regular closed concentric type, for the purpose of achieving plastic and organic integration with the specific physical context of the location, in some circumstances reaching complete mimesis with nature. In spite of this, the structure of the monastery, like that of a human biological system, symbolically reflects its Christ-centered character, the epicenter of all monastic life, in all its types, a character that in architectural form has remained unalterable for more than a thousand years in Greece and more than one thousand five hundred in the East, marking in this way the identity of Eastern Christian Monasticism for the Orthodox faith.

Both the architecture of the monasteries and the iconography that adorns a large part of their buildings, especially the *katholikón*, have been elaborated by means of a meticulous

---

[12] It is important to point out that the first thing that the monk or the monastic community builds is the place of worship and prayer, namely the church, and then the building program is completed, A Christian monastery without its main church would have no meaning as such.

[13] Within the range of types of Byzantine and post-Byzantine monastic architecture, we also find, in addition to the regular closed concentric types, other types such as the semi-open concentric, the compact, and the linear. See C. Conenna, *Monastic Architecture*, Chapter 2.2.2: "*Typology of Greek Monasteries*" p.178.

historical and theological study with a fine design in terms of both color and plan. This entirety, together with the architectural shape of the church's interior, creates a strong atmosphere of devotion, a space in which the aura of the Name of God is breathed, a redemption that assists the monks in their spiritual work: *prayer*. We refer to the prayer of Jesus, known also as the *"Prayer of the Heart"*, which is essential in Eastern Christian spirituality[14]. It seeks to find the spirit broken apart by the *"fall"* in the deep source of life, the heart. For this reason, it is no coincidence that the *katholikón* has a central place in the hierarchy of the monastic space and a different architectural expression, with a more refined design at all the levels of its resolution than the rest of the buildings of the monastery. Christ is the keystone of his church[15] and is present in the architecture like the heart in a living body[16].

---

[14] Meyendorff J., *Saint Gregory Palamás*, p. 40.
[15] «..*The stone that the builders threw away became the main stone of the building. That is the work of the Lord and left us amazed...*» Mt. 21:42
[16] Respiratory function, essential in the life of every organism, is tied to heart rhythm. For this reason, breathing the Name of Jesus is Life for creatures: "...*He is the one that gives all of us life, breath, and all things... for in him we live, move, and exist...*" He. 17:25-28.

Chapter 1

Ideas and Principles of Monastic Architecture

1.- The Idea of Monastic Architecture

The architecture of monasteries, both in the West and the East, reflects the essence of a style of life, that is, monasticism. In other words, monastic architecture as an artistic material expression "personalizes", as we could say in terms of the concepts of Plotinus[17], the content (the spirit) of monastic life. A significant part of the interest of this architectural topic is found in this mystic idea which expresses every monastery.

However, we believe that the architectural idea and the monastic conception of the Orthodox monasteries of the East differ from those of the Catholic monasteries of the West. These differences originate from a different dogmatic principle and continue with the different perception which each has of monasticism based on the same Christian principle: absolute dedication to God. On the one hand, there is the *"Hesychasm"* of the Orthodox Christians[18], which is represented in Byzantium by the Holy Fathers of the church and by St. Gregory Palamas (1296-1359)[19], which consider the nature of faith as "the prayer of the heart,"[20] and on the other, Catholic monasticism in the West, represented by St. Augustine (early 5th century), St.

---

[17] Plotinus, *Enneades*, "Beauty is not found in 'symmetry', nor in 'good coloring', but in the idea that the work expresses... A turning, then, from form to content... Everything has a soul, all the world is animate, and this soul, which is present in every material thing, is nothing but a reflection of the Mind. Thus, the material world is justified (through it we gain knowledge of the spirit). The work of art reflects material..." 4th-3, 4, 11.

[18] A. Guillou, *Civilisation*, pp. 389-390, 545.

[19] P. Christou, *Ecclesiastic Literature*, p. 44.

[20] J. Meyendorff, *St. Gregory Palamas*, p. 40. "Evagrios (†399) and Macarius, his teacher, defined all the essential elements of the later spiritual tradition of the monks of the East. The *mental prayer* of Evagrios will be in the later centuries, with Ioannis Klimakos, *pure prayer* as the purpose of hesychastic life..." *P.G.* v. 150, 1101-1122, and J. Serr, *Filocalia*, p. 187.

Benedict (early 6th century), and later, "scholastic theology."[21] Scholastic theology was expressed originally by St. Anselm (1033-1109) with his position that "belief is a work of intellect"[22], and later by St. Bonaventure (1221-1274), who refers to the "journey of the mind towards God" and finally, St. Thomas Aquinas (1225-1274)[23], who sustains that "the nature of belief consists exclusively of knowledge."[24]

With these concepts, we could sustain that the mentality, the way of thinking, behavior and concept of coenobitic monastic life of each culture (Byzantine and Western Middle Ages)[25] constitute points of reference in order to conceive the difference in the architectural idea between the Christian monasteries of the East and the West. By extension, the different manner of architectural expression helps us to understand the two cultures.

The Eastern Orthodox monasteries demonstrate a character of individuality: they are set, arranged, formed, and built more "organically", since the concept of their material implementation comes from sensitivity and the movement of the heart, while Western Catholic monasteries present a repetitive and collective character, and are attained and architecturally formed in a more "rational" manner, since the concept of their construction is based on strict logic.

"Organic" and "rational" (geometric) architecture differ in their conception in the following way: the basis of the "organic" conception is found in the idea of the building as a continuation of the plastic form of the natural environment, while the basis of the concept of "rationality" is found in the pure expression of geometric form. Although both concepts are in some way inspired by the form of nature, each finds morphological expression according to its own view concerning the image of

---

[21] J. Le Goff, *Civilisation*, pp. 246, 632-633, and C. Giannaras, *Planning*, pp. 151-165.
[22] St. Anselm, "Fides quaerens intellectum", see *P.L.* 158, 223.
[23] P. Christou, *op. cit.*, p. 122.
[24] St. Thomas Aquinas, *Summa Theologiae*, II-II.47.13 ad 2.
[25] A. Guillou, *op. cit.*, pp. 22-37. D. Talbot Rice, *Byzantines*, pp. 98, 124, 130-131, 138-141. J. Le Goff, *op. cit.*, pp. 421-428.

nature. Namely, while the former "imitates" the plasticity of nature by following it, the latter "assimilates" the basic morphological rules of nature as axes, shapes, etc. and expresses them geometrically. In other words, the monastery architecture of the East forms a figure which represents the idea of "natural expression", while the monastic architecture of the West constitutes the given morphological formation of a geometric model.[26]

More analytically:

> 1) Western monastic architecture expresses itself both in terms of the arrangement of spaces and volumetrically (in the expanse of its mass) with geometric shapes, with clear organization of volumes, and with axes of symmetry, forming in this way a rationalistic architectural conception of the monastery. The monastic architecture of the West, with this "rationalistic" expression, seems to follow, architecturally speaking, Western medieval logic, which is consummated in the pure schematic form of the theological thought of St. Thomas Aquinas, in his known work *Summa Theologiae*. Western monastery complexes show an inflexible typological evolution and a stricter morphological expression, where the order to which are subordinated dominates over the variety offered by the topic (monastery architecture) and often the site itself.
> 2) The Eastern monastic architecture of the Byzantine and post-Byzantine age, with almost the opposite perception, presents another logic for the composition of its buildings, the flexible logic of the heart, and as Blaise Pascal would say,

---

[26] A. Colquhoum, *Essays*, "... Form and Figure ...", p. 191, *"The term 'form' is related to the concept of geometry, while that of 'figure' is closer to the type..."*

"...the heart has its own logic, which knows nothing of logic..."[27]

The idea of this architecture expresses itself dynamically with invented organic shapes. We believe that these shapes are inspired by the figure of the setting within the natural environment and by the free architectural ideas of the *"founder-architect."*[28] Thus, the architecture of monasteries becomes organic and expressive, and variety dominates over order. In these monasteries, one can distinguish a lively and dynamic architectural character, both internally, in the form of the outdoor space, and externally, in their structured, fortress-like morphological structure. From these characteristics, we may consider the monastic architecture of Greece as a "romantic architecture", which does not mean architecture of the Romantic period, but romantic from the point of view that emphasizes the particular in relation to the general, the empirical in relation to the logical, and the concrete in relation to the abstract, which distinguishes itself for its multiplicity and variety and is characterized by an intense mystic atmosphere.[29]

In general, the Christian monastic architecture in Greece, with the formation of its volumes, expresses a result of growth, rather than of organization, as it recognizes the lively form of nature. By extension, the monastery appears as a topological space, rather than geometric space, according to the terminology of Christian Norberg Schulz for the romantic medieval settlement

---

[27] Blaise Pascal, *Thoughts* (277), p. 95.

[28] By "architect" we mean the sensitive, creative, and responsible person for the interpretation of the practical and psychological needs for the structure of his own habitation and that of those near him. The one who sincerely tries to express that architecture is not only construction, but also an idea, "the central idea" which adjusts itself simultaneously to the environment and the way of life (in this case, monasticism). R. Giurgola – J. Metha, *L. Kahn*, pp. 188-200. E. Kaufmann – B. Raeburn, *op. cit.*, pp. 280-281. Le Corbusier, *Vers une Architecture*, p. XXIII. A. Loos, *Ornamento*, pp. 221-222.

[29] Ch. Norberg Schulz, *Genius Loci*, pp. 69-71.

space, a space which indeed did not aim for regular, defined organization.[30] Additionally, the profile of the monastery, that is, its *"skyline"* presents, with its particular morphological structure, a romantic character similar to a medieval town, with its towers (the defensive tower and the bell-tower), the domes of its main church and chapels, as well as the structured walls.[31]

---

[30] Ch. Norberg Schulz, *op. cit.*, p. 69.
[31] Ch. Norberg Schulz, *op. cit.*, p. 70. *"The medieval town is a romantic settlement to an exceptional degree. The medieval town makes its presence visible with its towers and arrows, and its spaces are characterized by the sharp gables of its houses and the rich details without cause..."*

Monastery Dochiariou – Agion Oros

Monastery Dochiariou – Agion Oros

Monastery Dochiariou – Agion Oros

Monastery Stavronikita – Agion Oros

Monastery Stavronikita – Agion Oros

Monastery Stavronikita – Agion Oros

Monastery Peribleptos - Mystras

On another, more symbolic, side, we could say that in the various creative architectural ideas which are observed in the architectural expression of Byzantine and post-Byzantine monasteries in Greece, once again *"it is revealed"* that man was created in the image of God[32]. This element finds itself where human action, concerning creativity in the construction of a habitat, exceeds the bounds of logic, the static, and morphology and by extension, reflects the free way of action of God with His creations.[33] Thus, monastery architecture, with its composition, goes beyond simple functionality, the static nature of space, and the austere geometric expression of its volumes. In this way, we compare the human architect with the divine, meaning that the architectural inspiration and knowledge of the spiritual person, the *founder and architect*, concerning monastery art, in some way approached the unlimited inspiration and knowledge of God during the creation of the world.[34] With this concept, we can say that in Orthodoxy, the deep spirituality that characterizes man, corresponding to the creativity of God, and inspires him in his work, is *"Hesychasm."*[35] Therefore, we could state that the architectural expression of Greek Orthodox monasteries

---

[32] A.M. Allchin, *Man as image*, pp. 39-41.

[33] John 1:3-5, "*...everything came to be through Him, and without Him nothing came to be or happened. Life was in Him, and life was the light of mankind, and light appears in darkness and darkness did not overtake it...*"

[34] Romans 1:20, "*...those invisible things from the creation of the world are to be seen by those who create with thought...*"

[35] It should be noted here that according to J. Meyendorff the term "hesychasm" corresponds to four concepts: a) Orthodox spirituality (hesychia – ησυχία), b) the psychosomatic method of prayer ("the prayer of the heart"), c) the system of theological concepts known as "Palamism", and d) political Hesychasm, which takes the form of a social movement. See J. Meyendorff, *Hesychasm*, pp. 291-305, and *A Study*, pp. 134-157. With its broad meaning, Hesychasm can be considered a creative force and inspiration in the field of monastic architecture, as it is in art and literature. See A. Tachiaos, *Hesychasm*, p. 117.

originates from a *"pure creation of the spirit"*[36], which is emphasized even more in those monasteries which show an intense, separate architectural individuality[37] in their settings, the arrangement of their areas, and their morphological expressions. This architecture, which is set in a varied and difficult landscape but also answers in morphological terms in a creative, organic, and plastic way, emphasizes the basic knowledge of spiritual monastic asceticism in terms of buildings:

"... the spiritual man also benefits from adversity..."[38]

As a result, we may show in brief all the concepts which express monastic thought and the monastic architectural conception in the parallel routes of Western and Eastern Christianity in the following table:

Sketch of Monastery in the West

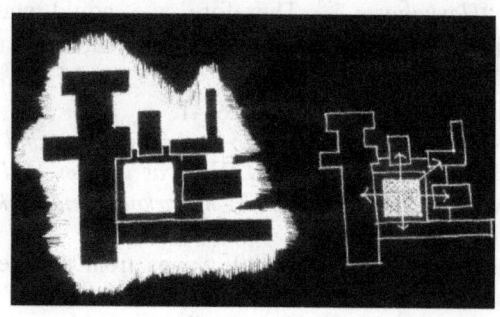

---

[36] Le Corbusier, *op. cit.*, pp. 129-131, 165-183. G. Simeoforidis, *Le Corbusier*, p. 103. We use the well-known concept of Le Corbusier (what he refers to the Parthenon as a *"pure creation of the spirit"*) to express this monastic architecture, an implementation of a purely spiritual way of life which is supported by the spirituality of the *"prayer of the heart"* of Christ and the fathers of the Orthodox church.

[37] C. Conenna, *Monastic Architecture*, chapter 3.1.2 "The monastery and the environment", pp. 328-333.

[38] T. Hambakis, *Gerontiko*, p. 384.

Characteristics of the monastic and monastery ideas in the West
- Saints Augustine and Benedict
- The Benedictine Rule
- St. Thomas Aquinas
- Scholastic Theology[39]
- Rationalistic logic
- Mind-based knowledge of God[40]
- Mind as center of human existence
- Imposition on the environment
- Criterion of repetition of the main idea
- Geometric setting (object)[41]
- Architecture of form[42]
- Strict geometric structure[43]
- Architecture of the model[44]
- Order dominates variety
- Homogeneity of form
- The «general» and the «abstract»
- International style[45] = dogmatic, systematic

---

[39] J. Le Goff, *Civilisation*, p. 632. "... Scholastic theology forms the dogmatic base of Western Christian tradition in the 12th and 13th centuries. Starting from the revealed Christian truths, it produces its conclusions with the principles and methods of scholastic philosophy...".

[40] S. Papadopoulos, *op. cit.*, p. 178. The center of human existence is the mind. The logical construction, with the function of knowledge and love, reaches God Himself.

[41] L. Hilberseimer, *Cities*, p. 133, 157.

[42] A. Colquhoum, *Essays*, "... Form and Figure ...", p. 191.

[43] Ch. Norberg Schulz, *op. cit.*, p. 71.

[44] G. C. Argan, *Typology*, pp. 564-5, and *Tipologia*, pp. 4-5. A. Colquhoum, *op. cit.*, p. 195.

Sketch of Monastery in the East

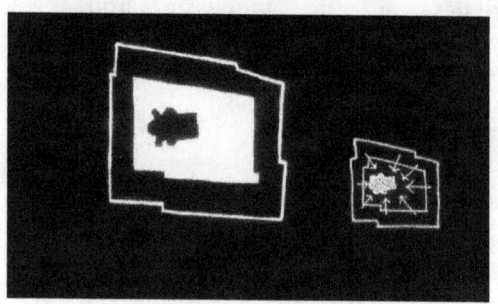

Characteristics of the monastic and monastery ideas in the East

   The Holy Fathers of the East[46]

   Hesychasm

   St. Gregory Palamas

   Theology of Divine Vision (Θεοπτία)[47]

   Experience of God or Theosis

   Experiential knowledge of God[48]

---

[45] H. Saalman, *Medieval Architecture*, p. 32. This is a type of architecture which has spread to all the Catholic world, with slight variations that provided the possibility of functioning in different climatic and cultural conditions, as happens in modern architecture. See also K. Frampton, *Modern Architecture*, p. 224.

[46] Grigorios Nazianzinos, Ephraim of Syria (4th cent.), Diadochos Fotikis (5th cent.), Ioannis of Klimaka, Maximus the Confessor (7th cent.), among many others.

[47] "Theology of Divine Vision is the periphrastic term which means the theory of God, that is, the vision of divine actions which are revelations of the divine essence...", S. Papadopoulos, *Meeting*, p. 174. See also Philip Sherrard, *The Sacred*, p. 125, "... in the Christian perspective human perfection is achieved through the theory / of viewing and how to view means to see God directly..."

[48] S. Papadopoulos, *op. cit.*, p. 177. The center of human existence is the heart. The entire human being, even physically, participates in the knowledge of the unconstructed actions of God.

- Heart as center of human existence
- Adjustment to the environment
- Criterion of individuality of main ideas
- Organic setting (contextual)[49]
- Architecture of the figure
- Romantic (topological) architecture[50]
- Architecture of the type
- Variety dominates order
- Heterogeneity of form
- The «individual» and the «concrete»[51]
- Local character = pluralistic[52]

These forms of categorization resulted from the analysis of the theological treatment and the architectural implementation of the Catholic and Orthodox Christian monastic institutions.

---

[49] M. Waisman, *Contextualismo*, pp. 83-84, and *Organicismo*, pp. 118-119.
[50] Ch. Norberg Schulz, *op. cit.*, p. 69.
[51] A. Kyriakidou-Nestoros, *Theory*, p. 27.
[52] Ch. Norberg Schulz, *Meaning*, p. 220. "The pluralistic spirit includes a wider purpose than does the systematic spirit, it goes further, and seeks, with the organic structure, the local forms and the local character, the meaning which forms the main human need..."

2.- Basic principles of composition

The topic of the design of the monasteries of the Byzantine and post-Byzantine eras in Greece presents a rich vocabulary of architectural concepts, with all the elements of space and form. For this reason, this architecture cannot stay at the margin regarding the general issue of architectural composition. It is important for us to integrate it in the context of the analysis of the basic principles which in some way define the organization of the art of architecture.

In the composition of monastery architecture during the periods studied, we may recognize some basic architectural principles of order, which allow us to understand the complete monastery design, the organization of spaces, the hierarchy of partial elements of the building program, as well as the total morphological solution for the monastery, as a construction. We consider these principles, in some way, as the techniques with which it is confirmed that *"multiform"* Greek monastery architecture contains an order in its conception. "Order without variety can end in monotony and boredom, but variety without order can constitute chaos."[53] In our analysis, we consider as basic principles of design of this architecture those principles which are "common denominators" in most monastery complexes, namely, the following:

- Flexible outline
- One architecture within another
- Rules
- Transformation
- Dominance
- Rhythm and repetition

---

[53] Francis Ching, *Arquitectura, forma, espacio y orden*, p. 332.

* The Flexible Outline

In the initial stage, we observe that the exterior monastery outline, that is, the walls of the complex, form a plastic-organic and flexible band, which, from the outer side of the wall, defines the shape of the monastery's ground plan, with uninterrupted continuity and by following the lines of the land. The exterior outline of these monasteries is presented in their ground plans in two ways: one occurs when the building is set parallel to the curves of the ground, where the lines of the outline appear with soft articulations and follow the shape of the land. The other way occurs when the monastery is set perpendicular to the curves of the ground, in which case the lines of the outline appear more crooked and step-like. In both cases, harmonious plasticity appears in the exterior outline of the monasteries, and organic flexibility appears in their ground plans, which come by principle from their way of being set, following and accompanying the slope of the ground in an unconstrained way:

"*Kinship of building with the ground. This basic inevitability in organic architecture...*"[54]

The internal outline of ground plans, from the side of the outdoor space, mainly follows, with minimal exceptions, the external outline of the monastery wall in parallel. That is, the parallelism of external and internal outlines becomes a principle for the formation of the wings in most types of monastic architecture (the enclosed, the semi-enclosed, and the linear).

At the second stage, we examine how the lines of these outlines are heightened and become views of the monastery, which take shape as building walls in the internal outline, oriented toward the internal outdoor space and as outer walls in the external outline, oriented toward the natural environment.

---

[54] Kaufmann – Raeburn, *Frank Ll. Wright*, p. 305.

Monastery Dochiariou – Agion Oros

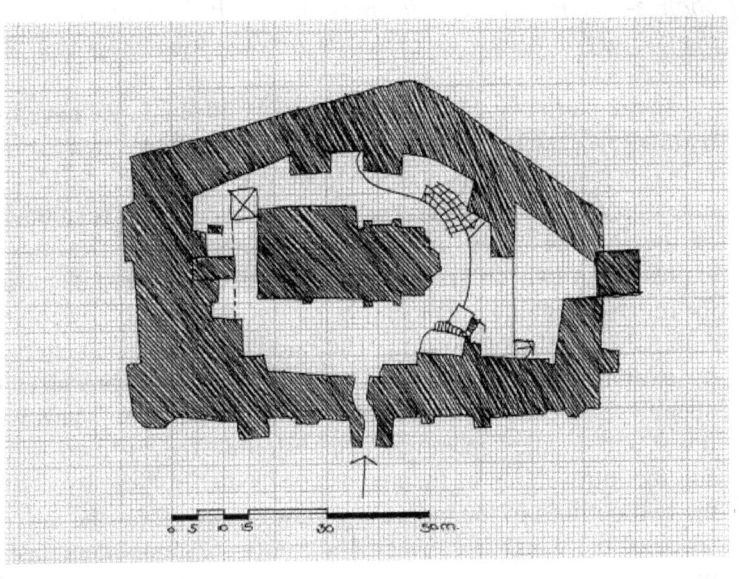

Monastery Dochiariou – Agion Oros

In his book *Complexity and Contradiction in Architecture*, Robert Venturi asserts that

> "...*Designing from the outside in, as well as the inside out, creates necessary tensions, which help make architecture. Since the inside is different from the outside, the wall -the point of change- becomes an architectural event. Architecture occurs at the meeting of interior and exterior forces of use and space...*"[55]

In the particular case of monastery architecture, we have two realities of external space: the internal outdoor area of the monastery, and the natural environment, which is outside the monastery. For this reason, the point of change in the relationship of the internal space of the wings and these two realities is expressed in two different ways: with the building wall toward the internal outdoor area and with the outer wall toward the external natural environment. The building wall is characterized by a more open articulation, with various types and sizes of openings and colonnades. In contrast, the outer wall is made with fewer and smaller openings, demonstrating the fortified nature and the introversion of the monastery theme. In these two ways, the two outlines of the monastery views express how the internal space of the wings is connected to the two external domains: to the internal outdoor space through the building wall, and to the natural environment through the outer wall.

The same thing does not happen with modern and contemporary monastery complexes. Speaking generally, they present both in their complete architectural order and in the organization of their building plan a clear academic design, which appears in their floor plans. This fact results from the placement of monastery complexes on normal landplots. These monasteries are designed in a rational and geometric way, following an austere and inflexible parallelism between the internal and external outlines in the wings of the monastery.

---

[55] R. Venturi, *Complexity and Contradiction*, p. 86.

* **One Architecture within Another**

Another basic principle of Orthodox Christian monastic architecture is the architectural emphasis on the Christ-centered view of the faith, enclosing the *katholikon*, the central place of worship, in the monastery complex. The *katholikon* is always contained and is placed inside the "*container*", the monastery building. In the coexistence of the two buildings, we observe that the *katholikon* is never larger in a volumetric sense, nor taller, than the rest of the monastery complex, and this is explained by the logic by which the contained element cannot be larger than its "*container*." However, we observe in the architectural relation of contained and container, in its respective dichotomy of *katholikon* – remaining the monastery complex, the coexistence of two opposed morphological concepts of order, the geometric and the organic, where the first is found within the second. The geometric proposal of the *katholikon* is found within the organic proposal of the remaining monastery complex. At this point of this analysis, it deserves noting that this is an expression of the characteristic dualism of opposites[56] of the congenital Greek spirit, which is continued in Byzantium.[57]

In the contained – container relationship, and correspondingly in the *katholikon* – remaining monastery complex relationship, we can distinguish two forms of "*containment*" of the *katholikon* in the monastery.

In the first, in which the *katholikon* is presented completely free in the monastic outdoor space, we distinguish three sub-categories, as we have already said: a) The internal outdoor space dominates the monument, b) Balance between the monument and the internal outdoor space, and c) The monument has a strong presence in the monastery's internal outdoor space.

The second form, on the other hand, shows the *katholikon* completely integrated in the (constructed) entirety of the

---

[56] John E. Hancock, "*On the Greekness of Greek Architecture*", pp. 285-296.
[57] P. Michelis, *Esthétique*, p. 276, and *Aesthetic Theorems*, p. 41.

monastery complex. This case is found in the monasteries of the *compact* and *unitary linear* types.

The *katholikon* is emphasized more as a "contained" element by its entire architectural shape, the articulation of its bulk, its structure, and its orientation, especially when it is placed free-standing in the internal outdoor space of the monastery. Its morphological differentiation, in comparison with the rest of the monastery, expresses its functional and symbolic importance as a dominant building, responding in terms of architecture to the most important issue of cenobite spiritual life, common prayer and worship.

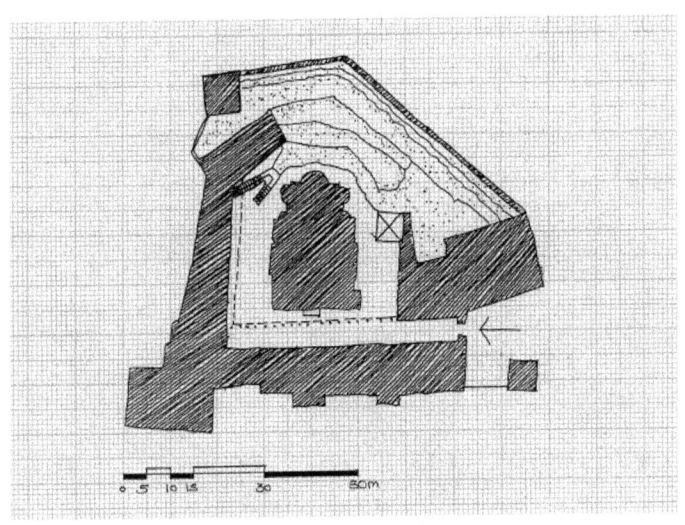

Monastery Ag. Pavlos – Agion Oros

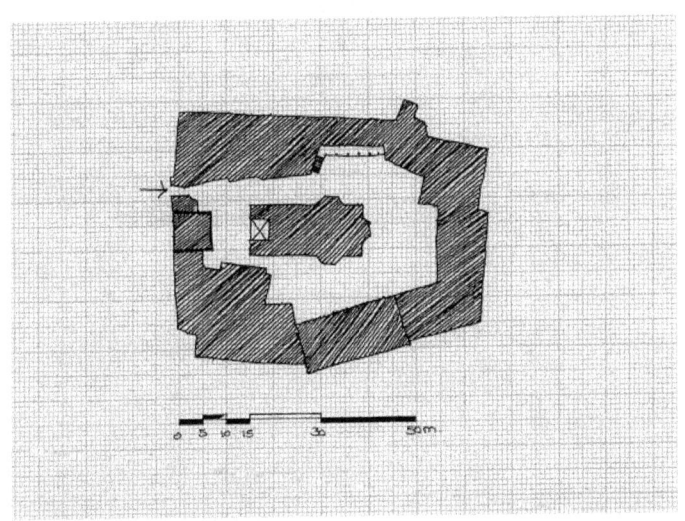

Monastery Karakalou – Agion Oros

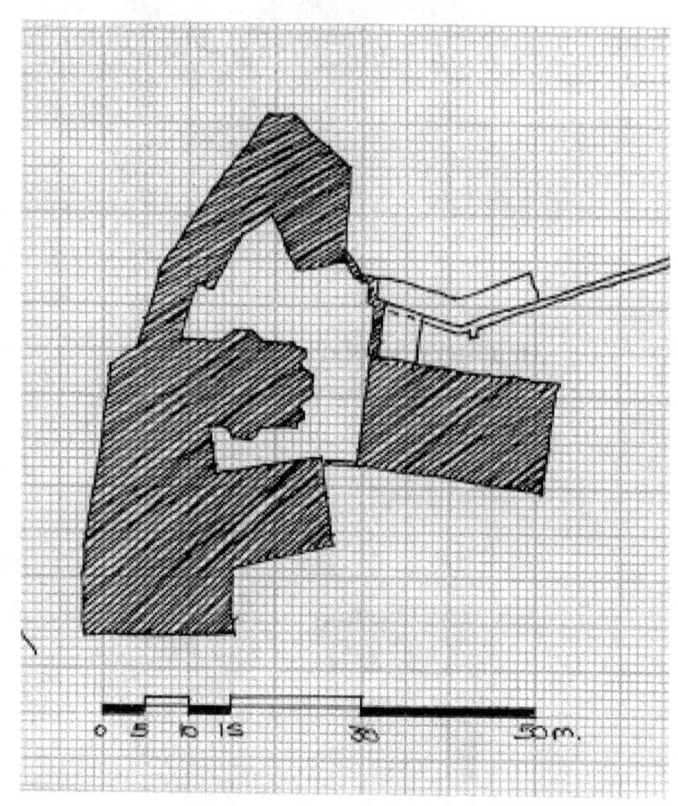

Monastery Simonos Petra – Agion Oros

Monastery Stavronikita – Agion Oros

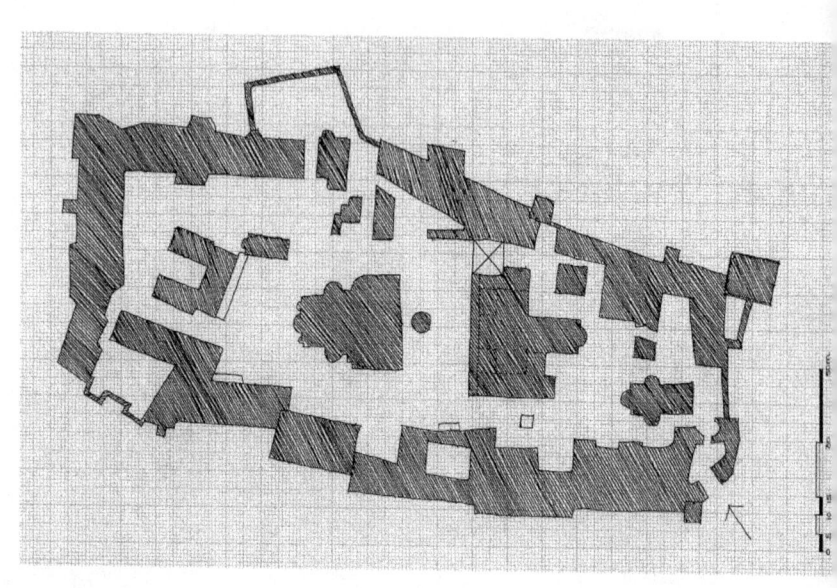

Monastery Megisti Lavra – Agion Oros

* The Rules

In architecture in general, the rule is a principle of order which organizes, distinguishes, and emphasizes the existing differences among its elements. This is a base, we could say, that gives the composition a visual cohesion, such as the symmetry of a pentagram, with its cohesion dominant, and a measure in a musical composition.[58] In the same way, we observe that in the composition of monastery architecture, there are various elements based on "rules", such as:

    a) Place, monastery type, and type of monastic asceticism, as the base of the monastery complex.
    b) The *zeitgeist*, as the base of the monastery's architectural language.
    c) Geometric composition, as the basis for the design of the *katholikon*, and
    d) An axis as base for the central monastic area of worship: *katholikon* and *refectorium*.

In further detail:

a) Place, monastery type, and type of asceticism as rules for the form of the monastery. According to the three forms of cenobitic monasteries (the regular cenobitic, cenobitic with ascetic tendencies, and the ascetic cenobitic), we observe two different cases applied in the construction of a monastery, which are determined by the importance attached by each group of monks to the founding of a cenobite monastery in the chosen place, for the appropriate type of cenobitic asceticism, and in the usual enclosed type of monastery.

Monastery Iviron – Agion Oros
1) The first case is the choice of the place and the "application" of the enclosed type. According to the large

---

[58] F. Ching, *op. cit.*, p. 358.

number of existing monastery complexes in Greece, we could say that the main principle which functioned as a general rule in the Byzantine and post-Byzantine era for the regular cenobitic monastery was the application of the regular Orthodox monastery architectural type, that is, the enclosed type.[59] This type was applied by following, naturally to the greatest possible extent, the lines of the plane of the selected setting, constituting in architectural terms an organic, enclosed, cenobitic monastery. One extreme application of this rule is seen in the later or modern monasteries, which maintain the basic rule of the enclosed type, but with rigorous academic regularity,[60] with austere geometry in its fortress-like bulk, and with axial symmetry in its entire morphological composition. The entrance to the monastery and the entrance to the *katholikon* are located in order along this axis, which coincides with the *katholikon*'s axis of orientation. We could say that the selection of place for these complexes is made exclusively for the application of the geometric enclosed monastery type.

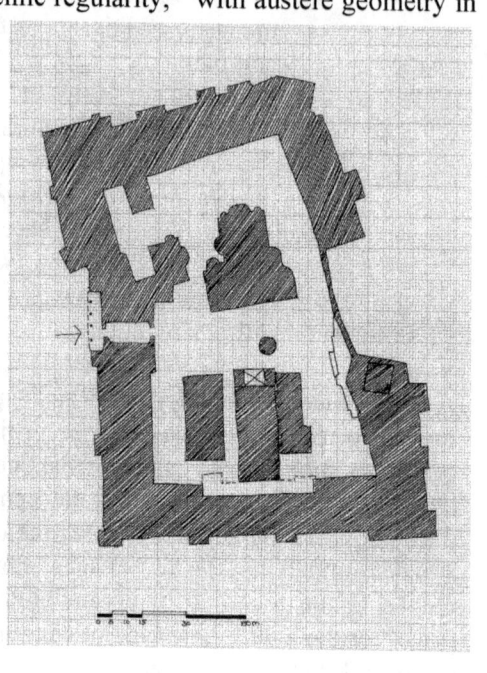

Monastery Iviron – Agion Oros

---

[59] C. Conenna, *Monastic Architecture*, Chapter 2.2.2: "*Typology of Greek Monasteries*" p.178.
[60] K. Papaioannou, *The Greek Monasterie*, pp. 28, 29.

2) The second case is the selection of place and adjustment of other architectural types. The other two forms of cenobite monasteries (the cenobitic with ascetic tendencies, and the ascetic cenobitic) follow, as a rule, the choice of a setting with more obstacles and difficulties, for a more specific asceticism on the part of the monks, where the founders adjusted another architectural type for monasteries, according to the possibilities allowed by the chosen site. Thus, we find the semi-enclosed and compact types in monasteries with ascetic tendencies, while we mainly find the linear type in purely ascetic monasteries. The regular monastery type could not be applied everywhere, because the specific chosen site is different from that of a regular cenobitic monastery.

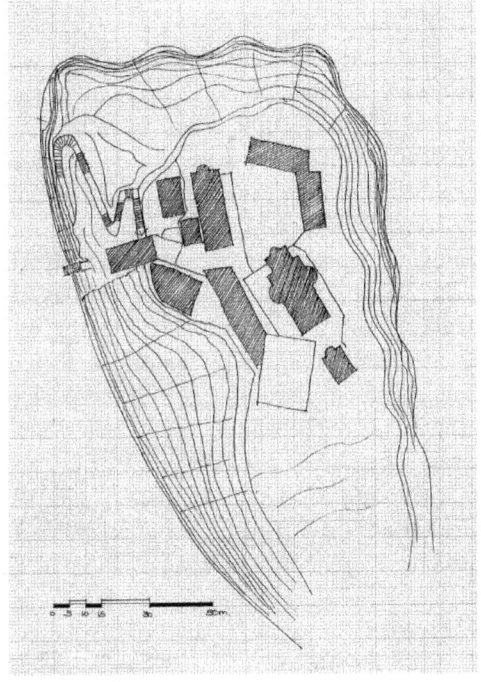

Monastery Megalo Meteoron - Meteora

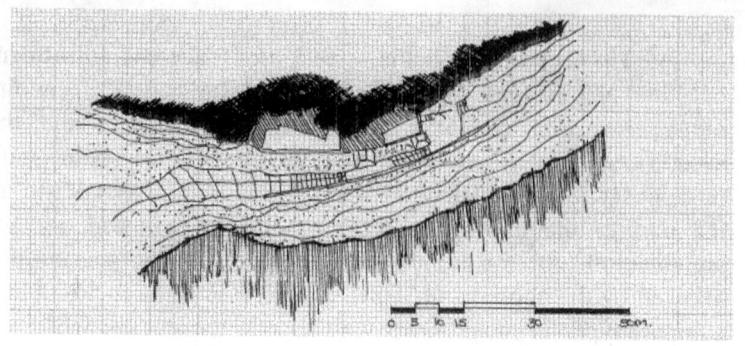

Monastery Hozoviotissa - Amorgos

b) The *Zeitgeist* as a rule for the monastery's architectural "language"

According to the age in which they were built or interventions were made, monastery buildings in Greece followed in some way the architectural spirit of each age, that is, the *zeitgeist*. We consider this as a rule because monastery architecture in Byzantium was characterized, like all the remaining existing architectural monuments of that era, by the detailed refining of the entire architectural form, the articulation of volumes, arches, domes, vaults etc., as well as the fine design of walls, openings, and decorations, and finally, by construction methods and materials, mainly brickwork and stonework.[61] On the other hand, monastery architecture in the period of Ottoman domination shows, especially in its most illustrious period (from mid-15th century to nid-17th century in all of Greece), according to the spirit of the era, a popular character, with aesthetic value and a picturesque nature.[62] These characteristics are observed in their morphological responses, construction methods, the ways that materials are used (wood, stone, and brickwork), details of construction (*tsatmás*, *bagdatí*), and the relative absence of

---

[61] C. Mango, *Arquitectura*, pp. 11, 12.
[62] M. Kambouri, *Church Architecture*, p. 178.

decoration, as we observe, for example, in the monastery complexes of Mount Athos.

Monastery Dionysiou – Agion Oros

Monastery Dionysiou – Agion Oros

c) The geometric volumetry of the *katholikon* as a rule for the composition of the monastery's space

Within the walls of the monastery complex, the most characteristic architectural element is the *katholikon*, which displays, especially in the monasteries of Agion Oros (Mount Athos), the most significant elements of Byzantine aesthetics: a pure geometric nature, a harmonious symmetry, and a well-ordered architectural composition.[63] These characteristics give form to one of the most usual and broadly applied types of monastery churches, the cruciform with a dome and lateral apses, the so-called Mount Athos or Athonite type. The dome, apses, and cross shape of the ground plan, along with the internal iconography, symbolically express the Orthodox dogma.[64] This architectural type conserves Byzantine tradition during the Ottoman period and follows the liturgical form of the Orthodox Church, which did not change with the fall of the Empire. Significant *katholika* of monasteries were built in Greece after the fall of Constantinople,[65] while keeping, in morphological terms, along with the geometry of their shape and the dynamism of their composition[66], their harmonic relationship with the overall volumetry of the monastery, both at the scale of an individual human and at that of the entire community of monks, which was always small and very rarely exceeded one hundred

---

[63] T. Steppan, *Lavra*, pp. 238-239, 241, 243, 248.
[64] G. Prokopiou, *Secular Symbolism*, pp. 119-120.
[65] E. Deligianni, *Survival*, pp. 41-47, and Ch. Bouras, *Byzantine Tradition*, pp. 154-156 "... Iviron, Dionysiou, Koutloumousiou, Filotheou, Stavronikita, Xenofontos, Doheiariou on Mount Athos, Megalo Meteoro, Agia Triada, Varlaam, and Agios Stefanos at Meteora, and also in Thessaly Agios Vissarion (Dousikou), Flamouriou, and others..."
[66] P. Michelis, *Esthétique*, pp. 80-83. The concept of dynamism is also discovered in the expression of shapes and forms in Byzantine painting, cf. *Ibid.*, p. 218, and P. Michelis, *Aesthetic Theorems*, p. 37., and M. Kalligas, *Aesthetics*, pp. 49-50.

monks.[67] Therefore, the size of a monastery church is not large, with the result that there is no *katholikon* larger than 800 square meters of floor area. Large *katholika* are observed only in large-scale monastery complexes, such as, for example, the monastery of Megisti Lavra or Vatopedi on Mount Athos. Other significant *katholika* are found in the following monasteries: Nea Moni on Chios (270 square meters), Osios Loukas in Fokida (450 square meters), and Osios Meletios on Mount Kithaironas (275 square meters).

Katholikon Monastery Megisti Lavra – Agion Oros

---

[67] C. Mango, *op.cit.*, p. 180.

d) An axis as rule for the organization of the center of worship

Another rule which is observed in monastery organization is the simultaneously longitudinal and centralized composition, which forms the basic principle of Byzantine church architecture. A similar composition is expressed in the monastery's subsystem of *katholikon*, court, and *refectory* (dining hall)[68], as it manifests itself in some monasteries on Mount Athos, namely Megisti Lavra, Vatopedi, Iviron, Koutloumousiou, Esfigmenou, and Ag. Panteleimon.

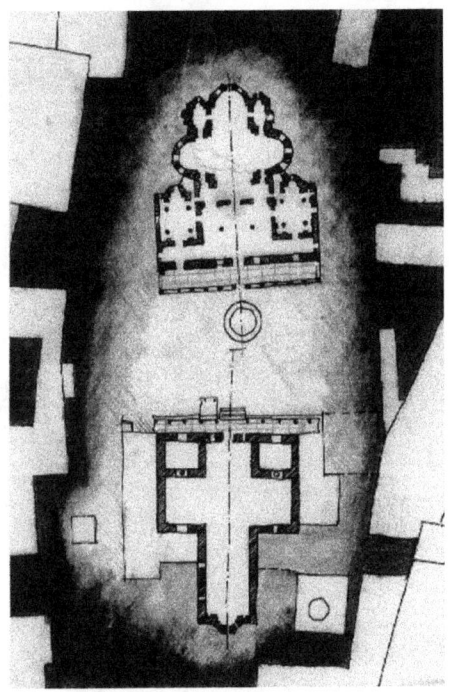

Monastery Megisti Lavra – Agion Oros

---

[68] C. Conenna, *Monastic Architecture*, Chapter 1.2.2: "*The Basic Organization of the Architectural program*" p.100.

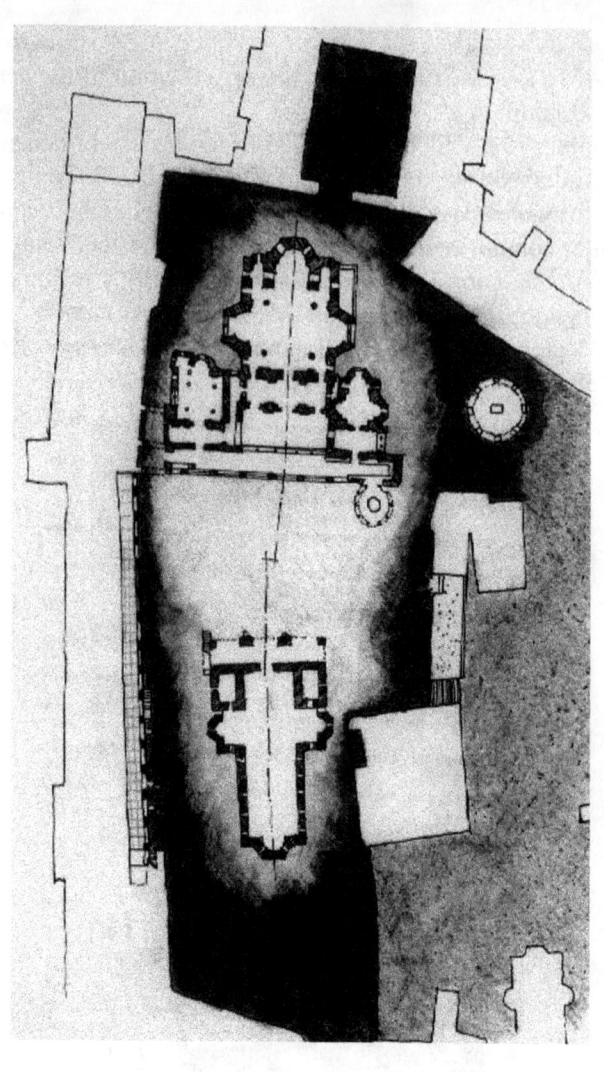

Monastery Vatopediou – Agion Oros

* **The "Transformation"**

The principle of *"transformation"* in architecture essentially contains the idea of change and alteration of form, but not of trans-substantiation, since it keeps a main idea in unchanged form, one which is transformed with some fine handling in order to provide specific responses to special conditions, whether functional or topographical.

The principle of transformation is observed in monastery architecture in three different cases:

a) The transformation of the monastery of the enclosed architectural type into a semi-enclosed one.
b) The transformation of the fortress type.
c) The transformation of nature.

a) The enclosed monastery type, which is mainly found in regular cenobite monasticism, is transformed according to the shape of the chosen setting which corresponds to the monastic activity, into a semi-enclosed or compact type of monastery architecture, for the placement and construction of the monastery. Thus, we could say that based on the principle of transformation, two architectural types for monasteries resulted. We also observe that in the same basic enclosed model for the regular cenobite monastery, a morphological transformation corresponding to the specific site of its setting takes place, the reason why all monastery complexes differ in terms of their ground plan.

b) The closed external fortress form which the monastery architecture of the Byzantine and early post-Byzantine eras followed was transformed and is still being transformed in terms of its volumetric character, by architectural interventions carried out in every age. The morphological transformations of volumes that took place in monastery architecture during the late post-

Byzantine era were enriched by the variety of new expansions and additions. In this way, the monastery was transformed as a building, became more extroverted, took on an almost urban architectural character, acquiring the multiform image of traditional architecture of a Greek town in its shapes, details of construction, materials, and colors. Therefore, the monastery ended up presenting a similar appearance to that of Thessaloniki in the facades and outer forms of its houses during the Ottoman period.[69] In this city, that is, in the upper city (Ano Poli), we find the shapes of traditional Macedonian architecture which visibly preserve the elements of Byzantine tradition, the human scale, and details of color, within the semi-enclosed shape of Byzantine walls.[70] The variety of this architecture is exemplified in many works of a diverse scale in the monastery complexes of Mount Athos.[71]

c) The transformation of nature results from the organic style of placement which, in general, occurs in all monastery architecture in Greece in the periods of time studied here. The concept of transformation is observed more, however, in some monasteries located on top of cliffs which extend their shape volumetrically. In this case, what is observed is a metaphorical transformation, in which the rock rises to its height and is transformed into a building. Five examples demonstrate this idea clearly: the monasteries of Simonopetra on Mount Athos, Roussanou, Agios Nikolaos Anapafsas, Agioi Theodoroi, Varlaam and Nea Moni in Meteora and Zoodohou Pigis in Kipinas.

---

[69] G. Velenis, *Historical Points of Change*, p. 19.
[70] N. Moutsopoulos, *Ano Poli*, pp. 7-31.
[71] P. Theoharidis, *Heritage*, p. 28.

This phenomenon consists of the architectural idea of transformation depicting monastic life metaphorically: an individual becomes a monk in order to concern himself almost exclusively with spiritual life and to make use of his spiritual gifts. In this way, he tries to be transformed from a human being into an essential person. This transformation corresponds symbolically to the Transfiguration described in certain texts of the Scripture.[72]

---

[72] *"And after six days Jesus took Peter, James, and John, and brought them to a high mountain where they were alone, and he was transformed before them, and his clothes shone white as snow, whiter than any fuller on Earth could whiten then..." Mark 9:2-3. "We all, mirroring the glory of God in our revealed visage, are transformed in the same image, from glory to glory, as if by the Lord's spirit..." II Corinthians 3:18. "... do not conform to this age, but transform yourselves for the renewal of your mind, to examine for yourselves what is the will of God, the good and pleasant and perfect..."* Romans 12:2.

Monastery Zoodohou Pigis – Kipinas

Monastery Zoodohou Pigis – Kipinas

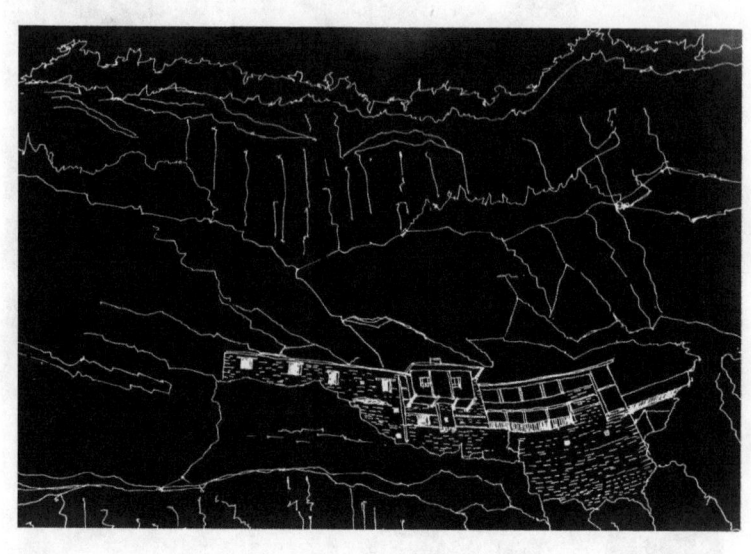

Monastery Zoodohou Pigis – Kipinas

Monastery Simonos Petra – Agion Oros

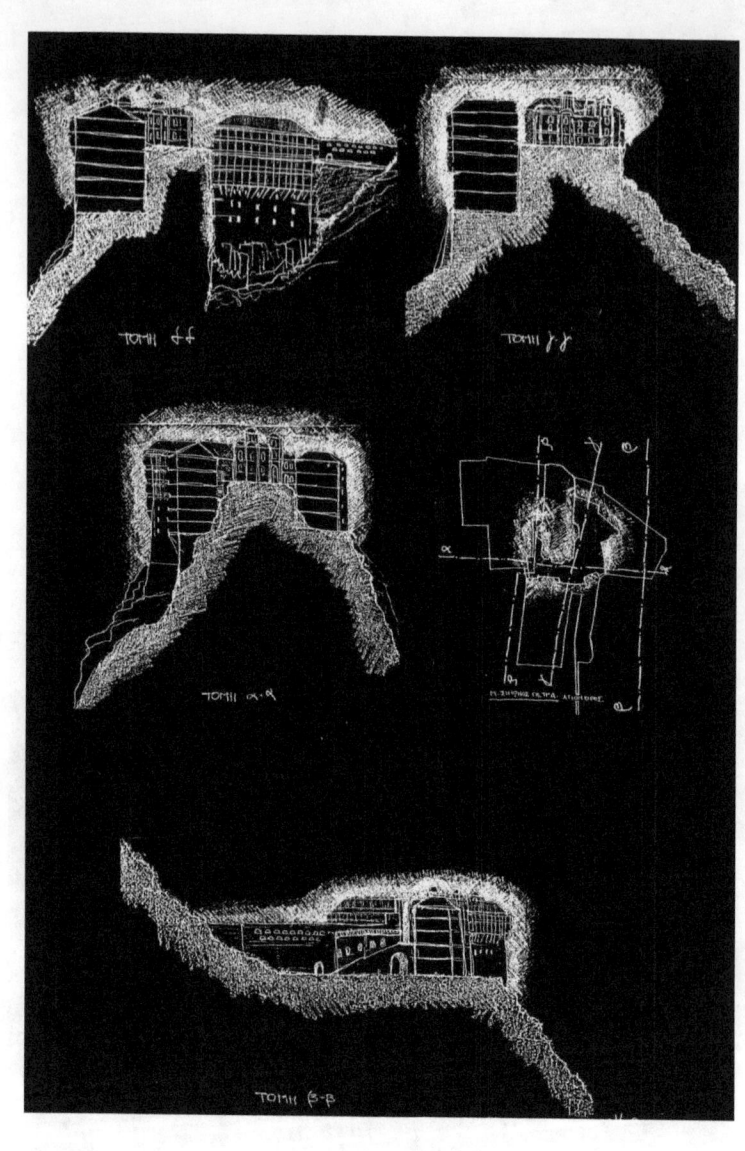

Monastery Simonos Petra – Agion Oros

Monastery Simonos Petra – Agion Oros

Monastery Nea Moni – Meteora

Monastery Nea Moni – Meteora

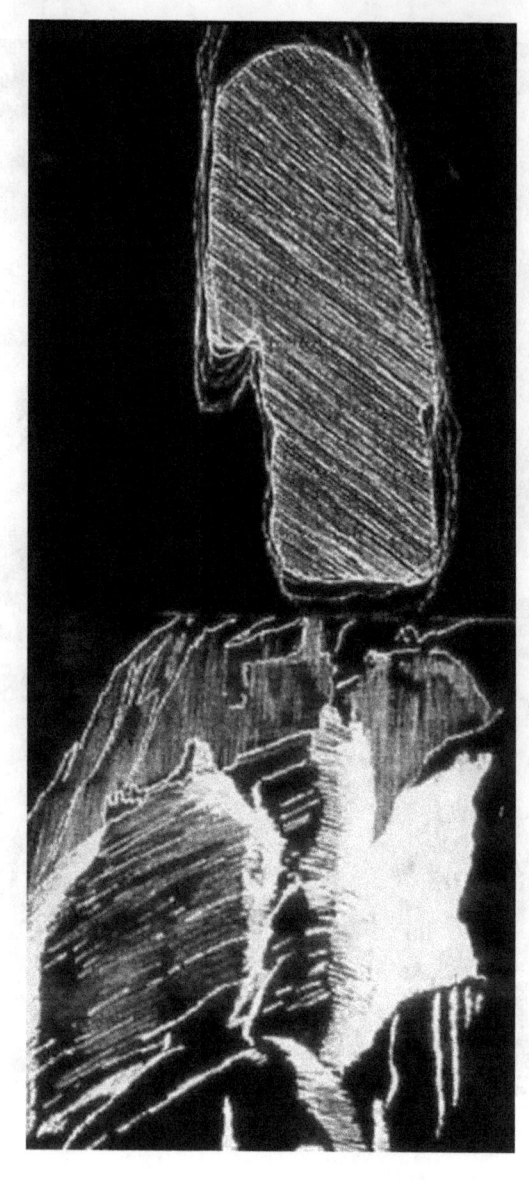

Monastery Nea Moni – Meteora

Monastery Nea Moni – Meteora

Monastery Ag. Theodoron

Monastery Varlaam – Meteora

* Dominance

The principle of dominance is meant in the architectural composition as an exception, which reflects in some way the level of importance of an element of the architectural plan, in terms of both its functional role and its symbolic one. This importance is expressed in dominant terms with form and volume, as well as a strategic placement in the ground plan of the entire architectural composition.[73] The principle of dominance is presented morphologically, functionally, and symbolically in monastic architecture, especially in the *katholikon*. This is expressed in terms of dominance with the clear outline of its form, its geometric composition, the harmony of its proportions, the plasticity of its volumes, the careful use of materials, color, and its placement in the monastery complex. In this way, the *katholikon* becomes, as a noteworthy building within the monastery's architecture, obvious, intense, and recognizable, expressing two topics both in architectural terms and symbolically: one general one, as an expression of Christian faith, *"the heavenly Jerusalem, the second paradise"*[74], and the second, a more specific one, as an expression of monasticism, *"the permanent memory of God."*[75] The architectural characteristics of the *katholikon* are emphasized even more in large-scale enclosed complexes, where the dimensions of the outdoor space allow a total *"perspective"* view of it.

---

[73] F. Ching, *op. cit.*, pp. 350-356.
[74] G. Prokopiou, *op. cit.*, p. 43, n. 132, where the source for this information is cited.
[75] T. Hambakis, *Gerontiko*, pp. 212-215.

Monastery Koutloumousiou – Agion Oros

The principle of dominance is also expressed with the presence of the defensive tower, where it exists, mainly in the monastery complexes of Mount Athos.[76] The dominance that the defensive tower presents in monastic architecture is essentially functional, as an observation post, and is expressed architecturally with its pure geometric form and volumetry, and its placement at the highest point of the landplot where the monastery complex is set.

Monastery Karakalou – Agion Oros

---

[76] C. Conenna, *Monastic Architecture*, chapter 3.1.2 "*Monastery Forms*" p.364.

Monastery Dionysiou – Agion Oros

* Rhythm and Repetition

"Rhythm is a situation of balance originating from simple or composite symmetries or from wise compensations. Rhythm is an equation: equality (symmetry, repetition); compensation (movement of opposites); modulation (development of an initial plastic invention)..."[77]

For the understanding of these two architectural principles, rhythm and repetition, which cannot be separated, it is important to explain the meaning of the concept of the recurrence model. This model helps the linear organization of a repetitive element of the building plan, which, set in a determined order along with the other elements, creates a rhythm. Rhythm generally refers to the regular and harmonic repetition of lines, outlines, shapes, or colors, helping the total organization of the shape and architectural space of a building with its substantial property of reiteration.[78] The principle of rhythm and repetition is especially present in the organization of monastery complexes with the cell as an element of the monastery's building program. The form, proportions, and size of the monk's cell make up the basic cell unit that affects the overall arrangement and formulation of the monastery. The ordered series of cells are arranged and grouped systematically, simply, and linearly. In the linear organization of the cells, we distinguish two types:

    a) "comb-type" linear organization, which is characterized by the arranging of the cells in a row that are served by an outer passageway, and

---

[77] Le Corbusier, *Vers une Architecture*, pp. 37-38. "... *Le rhythme est un état d' équilibre procédant de symmétries simples ou complexes ou procédant de compensations savantes. Le rhythme est une équation: égalisation (symmétrie, répétition); compensation (mouvement des contraires); modulation (développement d' une invention plastique initiale)...*"

[78] F. Ching, *op. cit.*, pp. 368-380.

b) "backbone-type" linear organization, which is made up of two rows of cells with a central corridor.

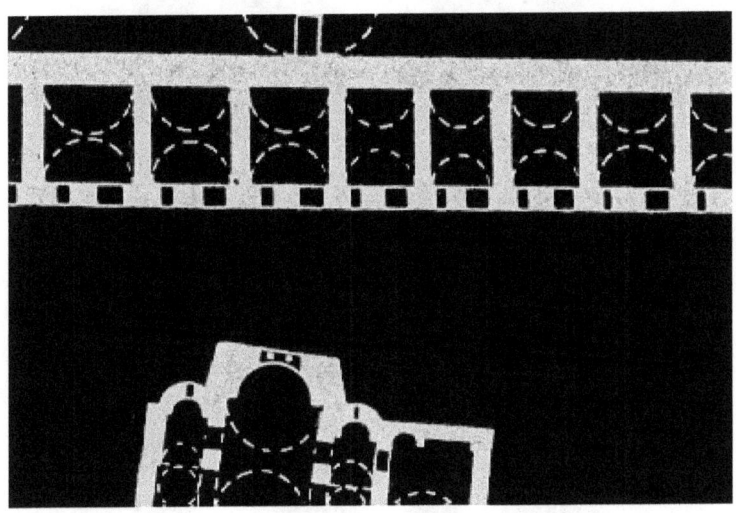

Monastery Osiou Meletiou – Kitheronos

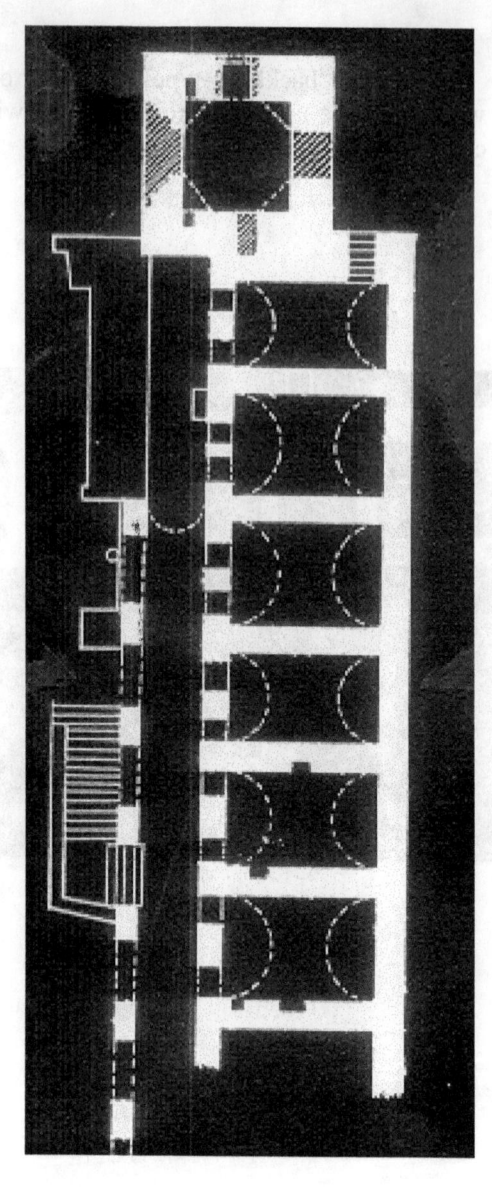

Monastery Osiou Louka - Fokidos

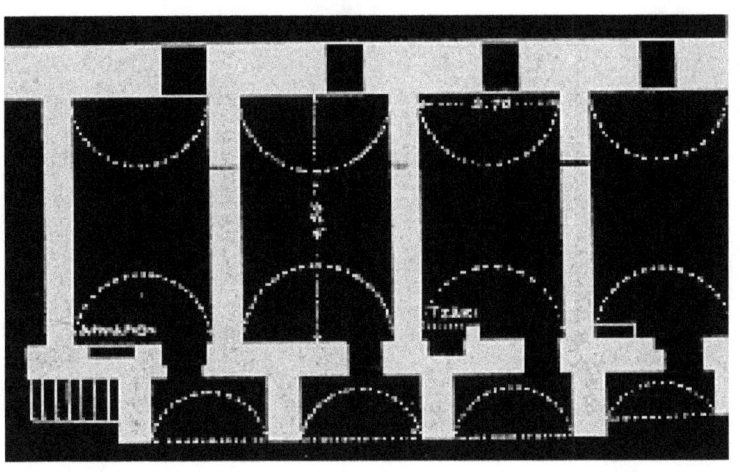

Monastery Ag. Ioannis Theologou – Patmos

Chapter 2

Morphology of Monasteries and Nature

The geography of Greece is characterized by varied forms of terrain, thanks to which holy monuments occupied the most attractive locations in antiquity and in the Byzantine Age.[79] The sensitivity of the Greeks regarding the choice of the proper site to evoke a mood of spiritual uplift and mysticism is well known.[80]

"...Topographically, Greece is formed by a determined variety of types. Each landscape is distinctly delineated. The intense sunlight and clean air contribute to the unusual presence of shapes..."[81]

In ancient Greece, before the construction of a temple, people set up outdoor altars at an ideal site from which the entire sacred precinct would be visible.[82] In the Byzantine era, monasteries were built on the site where the founder of the monastery lived, or near the cave where he lived in monastic isolation.

For Byzantine architecture, the view was a very important issue.[83] However, for coenobitic monastic architecture, the most basic spiritual issue was the selection of the site for monastic life.[84] Monasteries, of course, were closed to the outside and introspective, that is, they "looked" inwards, though the view did not cease to hold an important position. Their plastic architectural expression results from an interrelation with the terrain's morphology and leads to an organic-plastic system, according to which the introspective nature of the monastery does not invade nature volumetrically or morphologically. The creative and harmonious combination,[85] with which monasteries are integrated

---

[79] N. Moutsopoulos, *Gortynia*, p. 232.
[80] P. Mylonas, *Architecture*, p. 194.
[81] V. Scully, *Earth*, p. 9.
[82] V. Scully, *op. Cit.*, p. 45.
[83] G. Velenis, *Framework*, p. 34.
[84] D. Papachrysanthou, *Athonite Monasticism*, p. 66.
[85] S. Zafiropoulos, *Three Dances*, pp. 213-214, "The harmony of what is constructed with the natural environment... the natural environment and the constructed environment in their disciplined meeting, in their

in the environment, is the result of the sensitivity and respect for nature of the architects and founders.

The more ascetic a coenobitic monastery is, the higher are the mountains where it is established, and greater is its isolation. This course of monastic spirituality is a search for illumination of the heart, Divine Grace, knowledge of God, and the transformation of beings and objects,[86] that is the union of heaven and earth.

"...The marriage between heaven and earth forms the point of departure for the further differentiation of things. The mountain, thus, belongs to the earth, but it rises towards the sky. It is high, it is close to heaven, it is a meeting place where the two basic elements come together..."[87]

In general, the setting of monasteries during Byzantine and post-Byzantine times is mountainous, for two reasons:

    a)   Because Greece is in large part mountainous, and

    b)   Because monasticism requires isolation in order to ensure tranquility, as well as for reasons of protection, asceticism, and distance from worldly things.

The morphological and volumetric language of a large amount of Greek Byzantine and post-Byzantine monasteries speaks of a natural organic transformation of stone, which is elevated and is transformed into a work of architecture similar to the monk's elevation by means of his prayer to convert himself into a

---

good-natured communication..." and M. Le Caisne – J. Bouillot, *Sitio y entorno*, pp. 298-303.

[86] N. Matsoukas, *Byzantine Philosophy*, pp. 277-292, and V. Tatakis, *Byzantine Philosophy*, pp. 146-147.

[87] Ch. Norberg Schulz, *Genius Loci*, pp. 24, 25.

"person". Without being sculptures, these examples have a sculptural character, also possessing within them a richness of a higher order, spatial strengthening and continuity, created starting from the functional organization and resolution of the program's elements. The spatial quality of the interior of the monastery contains a mystical halo of interiority and introspection, sheltered within the folds of a great dynamic and variety of passages, corners, terraces, open patios, semi-covered areas, and galleries that are created between the *katholikón* and the wings of the monastery; extending, when the surface allows this, to the single buildings that there could be in the open area. This is a polysemy of labyrinthine dynamism similar to that of the human soul. These anonymous buildings for architectural culture enclose and safeguard, for the eyes of profound observers, an accumulation of real architectural wisdom just as the Lord keeps the essential secrets of life for the humble at heart because they are veiled by the apparent simplicity and humility of their implementation. In this arrangement, the builders of the monasteries often used materials from the neighboring areas, stone, brick, and wood, through which they expressed architectural sincerity.

Thus, sincerity, as a basic rule within coenobite and monastic Christian life, is transferred materially to the expression of its own architecture. The simple shapes and typology of the elements that constitute the monastery's program vary in their dimensions and proportions in accordance with the space available for the building of the monastery. In any case, it depended on the site of its location and the physical context, which on more than a few occasions, defines a specific scheme for the monastery. It is necessary to add that the formal variation that developed over time in many monastery complexes also depended on the demographic evolution of the monastic community.

The groups of coenobite communities such as the monastic community of Mount Athos (Halkidiki) or that of Meteora (Thessaly), or the community of Gortynia in the Peloponnese, are emblematic examples in the territory of today's Greece of the theological thoughts translated into architectural language that we are still developing. Each one, in a rather different way, exhibits in architectural terms a specific trend within monastic forms. We specifically avoid speaking of monastic orders, since in Orthodoxy this group concept does not exist as it is accepted by the monasticism of the Christian West, but it is more effective for our understanding to differentiate them based on the locations and forms of placement of the monasteries, which gives us the rule for a specific way of monastic asceticism.

The community of Agion Oros, on the peninsula of Mount Athos, clearly shows its coenobite direction, as such, with its respective characteristic typology. The community of Meteora, in the monumental *"forest of rocks"* of Thessaly, suggests a coenobite monastery inclined towards asceticism, since it implies a more individual and organic architectural response due to the natural conditions of the terrain[88]; while in the monasteries of Gortynia, which lie on the slopes of the mountains that form a deep valley above the Lousios River, indicate their more ascetic than coenobite character, and the architectural response in general imposes linear spatial organization, and in morphological terms, a stone curtain wall enclosed a naturally formed cave in the rock, in which the life of the monastery takes place.

This plastic and organic architectural response of the coenobite communities mentioned above, which adapt to the physical conditions of the land and engage in dialogue with nature, intervening in it with subtlety and respect, leads us to sustain as a concept that in Greek Byzantine and post-Byzantine monastic architecture, human language, *art*[89], communicates and meets the language of God, *nature*[90]. Dialogue and representation are the form of communication and meeting: dialogue between God and man, between created nature and creative art, manifestation of God by created nature, and of man by means of creative art.

---

[88] The area of Meteora is characterized as resembling a forest of gigantic rocks, on whose summits the monasteries are located, like the crowning level of a tower.

[89] Scully V., *L. Kahn*, p. 36 and Giurgola R. - Metha J., *L Kahn*, p. 34.

[90] Serr J., *Filocalia,* p. 25.

The Monastery and the Environment
(an organic dominance)

The Christian monastic form, we could say, is the result of the interaction between two forces, the material and the spiritual. Each monastery, both in the East and the West, has its own character and physiognomy, which, in its architectural form, consequently manifests the character and physiognomy of the group of monks who built it. The factors that essentially determine the morphological characteristics of the monastery are the following: first, the nature of the site where the monastery is set; secondly, the relation the site has with the landscape, of which the monastery forms a part, and thirdly, the topographic characteristics and climatic conditions. On the other hand, the morphological physiognomy of the monastery complexes is characterized by the creative architectural expression of the spirit of the founders and monastic or lay "architects."

We can separate the morphological architectural expression of Christian monasteries, along general lines, into two types, the geometric and the organic. Western monasteries belong to the formal, and Eastern monasteries to the latter. Historically, the two concepts[91] evolved in the following way: by *"geometric"* we mean the Roman order, which takes into account need and function and above all depends on a general dominant form concept which it follows in any setting. In contrast, the Greek order is considered more optical and *"organic"*: with its own rule for each case, it is more natural and autonomous in character. The geometric form ignores the characteristics of the site, and by extension it comes into conflict with the landscape, while the organic is a part of the site and harmonizes itself with the landscape. The geometric form, with its superimposing character made up of strict lines, is implemented in competition with nature, which does not recognize straight lines. The geometric form imposes itself on nature, in contrast to the organic, which

---

[91] L. Hilberseimer, *Cities*, p. 133.

adjust itself to topographic variety, by recognizing and using the particularities of the terrain. The organic form also recognizes the interrelation which exists between man and the environment, of which the former, ecologically speaking, constitutes a part. With this conservative spirit that dominates everywhere, the organic designer knows that nature has a beauty of its own, where careful intervention must achieve pictorial values; thus the building, in harmony with nature, uplifts its value. In this particular case we could support the following statement: whatever is a disadvantage for the inflexibility of the geometric shape is an advantage for the flexible organic form, which becomes capable, with its irregular plasticity, of surpassing any setting.

Monastic architecture in Greece during the Byzantine and post-Byzantine era promotes a close and well-adjusted relationship with the multifarious natural environment of its setting. In this sense, we can consider it *"organic"*. The *"organic"* architectural integration of the monasteries with nature is the expression of the continuity, in another language, of the ancient Greek organic architectural tradition, as well as the respect and humility based on Orthodox Christian faith, according to which the monk is considered responsible for an intervention within nature.

"... as a priest and celebrator of liturgy, dominator and handler of nature, he does not forget that he has the duty to present it and exalt it before the Creator..."[92]

The organic integration of this monastic architecture in nature symbolically reflects the integration with which the spiritual human *"sinks"* into God, in order to form a total unity with Him and to be in harmony with Him.[93] In other words, we may say that the organic integration that Greek monasteries show in their

---

[92] T. Papagiannis – Father Eliseos, *Natural Space*, p. 20. See also A. Loos, *Ornamento*, p. 232: " *...human work must not compete with the work of God ...*" and I. Zizioulas, *Creation*, pp. 44-46.

[93] A. M. Allchin, *Man as Image*, pp. 36-48.

specific setting is not simply external, but originates from the interior of the building, from the reason why it was built, namely in order to *"cover"* the coenobitic monastic style of life. This natural integration reflects the life of every monk, who *"builds"* his internal integration in order to belong to the nature of his own existence, his brotherhood, and his Creator. In this way, monastic life takes monastic form in a natural way.

The organic monastery form in Greece is called *"natural"* since it consists of an architecture of nature for nature, which is inspired by the natural landscape to which it adjusts, following the form of the ground, and is exalted architecturally in the form of a monastery in order to be harmonized with it. The quality of integration depends on the use of the construction materials used in building the monasteries. The natural characteristics of each (stone, brick, wood) are kept in their entirety, in order to give the buildings their true, "organic" architectural expression.

At this point it deserves noting that the means of translation of monastic life into monastic architecture finds exemplary expression in specific monastery buildings. A similar architectural expression is found in the thoughts and the philosophical approach of the well-known modern American architect Frank Lloyd Wright (1869-1959). His principles concerning architectural philosophy, organic architecture[94], integration of the building in its natural environment[95] and the proper use of the nature of materials[96] were translated architecturally in a very authentic way, and at an earlier time, in the anonymous monasteries which we are studying here. The purpose of this comparison between the Orthodox monastic architecture of Greece and the philosophy of architecture of Frank Lloyd Wright is not based solely on the coincidence which

---

[94] Frank Lloyd Wright, *Organic Architecture*, p. 47, and E. Kaufmann – B. Raeburn, *Frank Lloyd Wright*, pp. 233 and 304-5.

[95] Frank Lloyd Wright, *Natural House*, pp. 121-123. and E. Kaufmann – B. Raeburn, *Frank Lloyd Wright*, pp. 272, 292-296. Robert McCarter, *Fallingwater*.

[96] F.L. Wright, *op. cit.*, pp. 52-53. E. Kaufmann – B. Raeburn, *op. cit.*, pp. 222-229, 321-2.

exists between them, but mainly on the importance of the architectural treatment of the philosophy or rather the theory of the globally recognized architect in Greek monastic architecture of the Byzantine and post-Byzantine eras. This architecture gives specific form to what Wright "discovered" or "developed" many centuries later, as a new way of thinking for architectural design. It is our view that Wright himself did not know these monastic examples which concern us, but his recognized theory and works prove the qualitative particularities of this architecture. Thus, we could also say that the use of reinforced concrete in his work did not allow him to "express" his rich and interesting theory, which in the end formed a rational organic syntax of architecture within the natural environment, authentically and genuinely. Rational, in the concept of the geometrical rhythmic refinement of architectural space in his works. Organic architecture, as Wright defines it, surpasses the natural level of construction in order to express the meaning of spiritual creation.[97] As the monastery complex is integrated organically within the natural environment where it is set, it gives the impression that some spirit (the Holy Spirit) guided and helped man with both the selection of the location for its setting and the idea of constructing the monasteries, which form, in the final analysis, wonderful architectural work, such as the following monasteries:

- Kalamiou (Gortynia)
- Filosofou (Gortynia)
- Ioannis Prodromos (Gortynia)
- Roussanou (Meteora)

---

[97] E. Kaufmann – B. Raeburn, op cit., pp. 277-281. (17) Kaufmann E.- Raeburn B., op.cit., pág. 277-281 "...*architecture is life; or at least it is life itself taking form and therefore it is the truest record of life ... architecture I know to be a Great Spirit. It can never be something which consists of the buildings which have been built by man on earth... Architecture is that great living creative spirit which from generation to generation, from age to age, proceeds, persists, creates, according to the nature of man, and his circumstances... architecture is a necessary interpretation of such human life as we now know...*"

- Agios Nikolaos Anapafsas (Meteora)
- Nea Moni (Meteora)
- Agioi Theodoroi (Meteora)
- Simonos Petra (Mount Athos)
- Agios Pavlos (Mount Athos)
- Dionysiou (Mount Athos)
- Zoodohou Pigis (Kipina)
- Hozoviotissa (Amorgos)

The architecture that is represented by the above buildings could be said to surpass the natural level (of construction, material, and form), expressing a spiritual or supernatural energy that interprets monastic life, the nature of the human monk and the conditions of his life. In order to understand better the concept of supernatural energy in man, it is useful to see what St. Gregory Palamas says on this topic:

> "... Among the gifts of God, some are natural: they are offered to all without distinction, before the Law, under the Law, and following the Law. Other gifts are supernatural, spiritual, and completely unapproachable. I consider the latter gifts superior to the former, just as those who were judged worthy of the wisdom of the Holy Spirit are superior to the entire group of Greek philosophers. Further, I say that one of the natural gifts of God is philosophy, as well as the discoveries of human reasoning, the sciences..."[98]

---

[98] J. Meyendorff, *St. Gregory Palamas*, p. 134.

Monastery Ag. Nikolaos Anapavsas – Meteora

Monastery Ag. Nikolaos Anapavsas – Meteora

Monastery Ag. Nikolaos Anapavsas – Meteora

Monastery Ag. Nikolaos Anapavsas – Meteora

Monastery Roussanou – Meteora

Monastery Roussanou – Meteora

Monastery Roussanou – Meteora

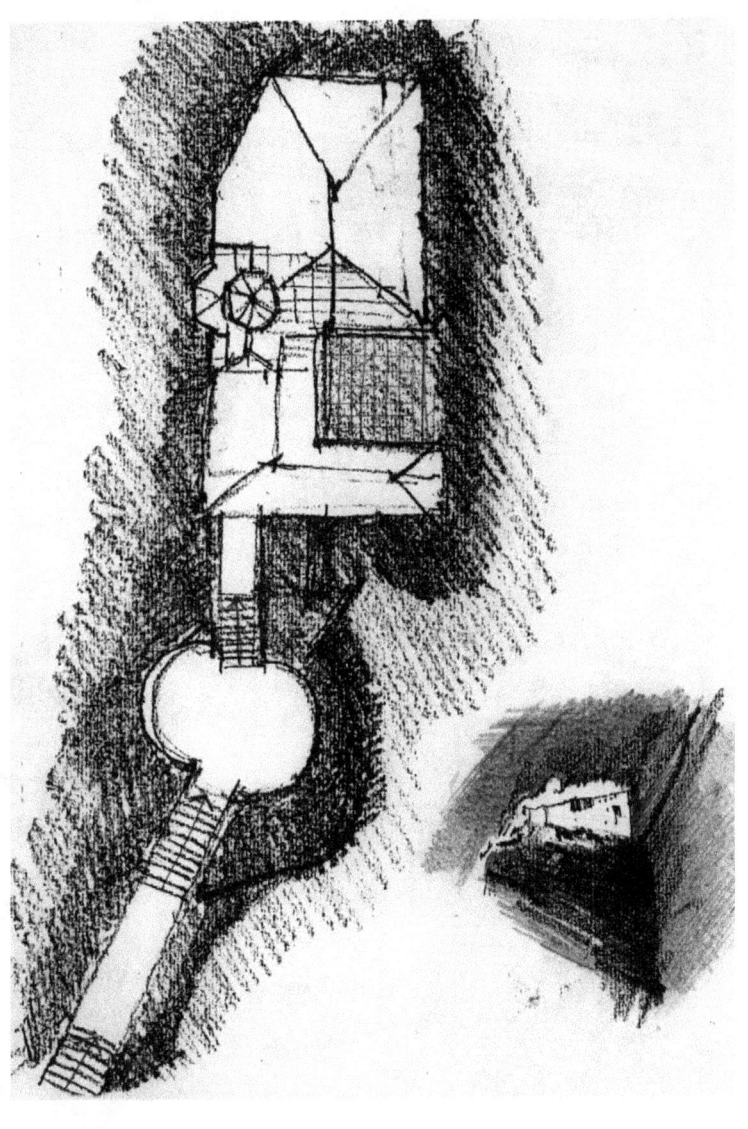

Monastery Roussanou – Meteora

Monastery Dionysiou – Agion Oros

Monastery Dionysiou – Agion Oros

Monastery Dionysiou – Agion Oros

Monastery Dionysiou – Agion Oros

Monastery of Simonos Petra – Agion Oros

Monastery of Simonos Petra – Agion Oros

Monastery of Simonos Petra – Agion Oros

Monastery of Simonos Petra – Agion Oros

Monastery of Simonos Petra – Agion Oros

Monastery of Simonos Petra – Agion Oros

Monastery Hozoviotissa – Amorgos

Monastery Hozoviotissa – Amorgos

Monastery Hozoviotissa – Amorgos

Monastery Hozoviotissa – Amorgos

Monastery Hozoviotissa – Amorgos

Monastey Philosofou – Gortynia

Monastey Philosofou – Gortynia

Monastery Ag. Ioanni Prodromou Gortynia

Monastery Ag. Ioanni Prodromou Gortynia

The Façades

With respect to the composition of the monasteries' façades, we note that it comes out to be, over time and with its constant adjustment to changes in technology, a complex, dynamic, and varied design, in which small volumetric schemes are inserted as an expansion of the interior, with different materials and colors. However, in most cases we notice a certain order of composition, in which the relationship between the *background* and the *figure* appears clearly. The internal façades of the monastic precinct, which face the *katholikón*, are presented in the form of the curtain of a perforated scenic background, due to the presence of continuous galleries, while outwards, the background appears compact, with the image of a fortress at its base and lighter varied and alternating shapes of outstanding volumes at the higher levels. These interventions of the post-Byzantine age give the image of the monastery an eloquent three-dimensional plasticity on its outside.

The varied cross-section, combined with the plastic organization of the floor plan and the dynamic one of the intermediate spaces, the architectural scale of the monastic buildings – always at a human scale – the introverted space, the articulated façades, both the very perforated interior one and the compact and semi-closed exterior one, lead us to the idea of a refuge and a fortress full of internal life, which, on the other hand, become a representation of God for a monk:

> "...*The Lord is my rock, my fortress, and my liberator. O my God! The rock in which I seek refuge, my shield, my strength, and my salvation!...*" Psalm 18:3

Monastery Iviron – Agion Oros

Monastery Dochiariou – Agion Oros

Monastery Vatopediou-Agion Oros

Monastery Stavronikita-Agion Oros

Monastery Xenofontos – Agion Oros

Monastery Ag. Theodoron – Meteora

Monastery Ag. Theodoron – Meteora

Monastery Megisti Lavra – Agion Oros

Monastery Philotheou – Agion Oros

Monastery Ag. Ioanni Prodromou - Serres

Monastery Ag. Ioanni Prodromou - Serres

Monastery Ag. Ioanni Prodromou - Serres

Chapter 3

Modern Architectural Thought as a Means to Approach and Interpret Monastery Architecture

Monastery Architecture

With today's conditions in hind, how timely monastic architecture can be is made apparent by the views and work of great modern architects such as Louis Kahn (1901-74), Alvar Aalto (1898-1976), Le Corbusier (1887-1965) and Frank Lloyd Wright (1869-1959). In this way, the architecture of monasteries in Greece acquires an even greater interest and timeliness for modern civilization.

Especially interesting is the fact that the ideas that characterize monastery architecture are found in the philosophical approach to architecture of Louis Kahn. This pioneering architect, who although he is classical in terms of the stability and symmetry of the shape of his buildings, simultaneously, because of the means of construction, appears as a romantic, with nostalgia for the Middle Ages.[99] His thoughts on *Silence* and *Light*[100], where the spirit of his architectural work can be found, could be described as valid for the essence of the spirituality of monastic life, as well as for the actualization of the monastery.

Kahn researches architecture as an expression of place for man in the world, at all levels: the social, the aesthetic, and the spiritual. In his research, the great importance of human institutions is emphasized: they express human desires in the constructed environment.[101] For Kahn, desire is the "avenue" of expression and the cause of life. In this way he distinguishes

---

[99] K. Frampton, *Modern Architecture*, p. 215.

[100] According to Kahn, silence is the principle of art and of any work of art. Light is the original source of all natural rules and the giver of presence. Silence creates or expresses something and light gives it shape. Silence expresses the unmeasurable; light, the measurable. Matter, on the other hand, is the erased light. R. Giurgola – J. Metha, *Louis Kahn*, pp. 15-17 and J. Lobell, *Louis Kahn*, p. 20.

[101] By "institution" Kahn means the desire of the human being, implemented as architecture. Institutions come from the inspiration of living. J. Lobell, *op. cit.*, p. 44, 65 and R. Giurgola – J. Metha, *op. cit.*, pp. 93-96.

three basic human desires: the desire for learning, the desire for contact with fellow humans, and the desire for human well-being.[102] According to Kahn, the school, for example, is a place in which the human desire for learning is satisfied. Correspondingly, we could similarly accept that the monastery is not simply a place that houses monks, but is a place where their desire to "learn" the will of God and the road to salvation is fulfilled.[103] Their desire for contact is covered by the coenobitic nature of monastic life. The desire for well-being is covered by the effort to become acquainted with God and to dedicate their life to Him completely in one place: the monastery, where human efforts for the salvation of the world are gathered. The completeness of its construction, its functionality, the quality of its areas, and the aesthetic that characterize the monastery area correspond to the basic human desires, as they are understood in the spiritual context of monastic life.[104]

It is also important, in order to understand where the philosophy and work of Kahn meets monastic architecture, to know the concepts that Kahn himself expresses regarding architectural setting and space and how they are implemented in his work. For Kahn, architecture begins when man, while researching his activities, decides *where* he will place the building for their development. Thus the concept of *place* is born: man creates a space there, where he carries out his activities and in fact declares his existence and essence.[105] The spirit and desire to live in a specific manner are found in the nature of this space.[106] This logic explains the architectural shapes "created" by Kahn, in which the familiarity of internal spaces is emphasized, the concept of human well-being is increased, and a separate, expressive architectural "language" is

---

[102] J. Lobell, *op. cit.*, p. 66, R. Giurgola – J. Metha, *op. cit.*, p. 34
[103] *"Teach me to do Thy will, for Thou art my God..."*, Psalm 142:10
[104] The monk, before entering the monastic community, has the possibility to choose the monastery that leads to his repose (the one that fits with his character and monastic leanings).
[105] R. Giurgola – J. Metha, *op. cit.*, pp. 53-54.
[106] V. Scully, *Modern Architecture*, p. 113.

constructed. In all his work, one observes a gradual transition from noise to silence, from light to penumbra, from common areas to private areas, always in search of human well-being. His buildings have very often been conceived as closed and compact units, which prevent anyone from "guessing" what takes place inside, creating a secret enigma at the same time.

Monasticism, which seeks introspection, silence, and isolation for the repose of the soul of the monk, expressed itself architecturally, since the Byzantine age, with the creation of a remote monastery setting, closed and secret, with a compact, bulky character and a plastic morphological articulation. These ideas, both the philosophical and the architectural (except for geometric expression) correspond to the work of Louis Kahn[107] at both the spiritual and the practical level.

Monastic architecture in Greece is *functional*, with reference to the use of the building, and at the same time *organic* in terms of the harmonious adjustment of the building to the natural environment. Thus, we could say that it constitutes a flexible synthesis that expresses the freedom of the truth of the Christian spirit plastically and artistically. We find a similar architectural approach, both functional and organic, in the work of Alvar Aalto.

Harmony and cultural heritage are two concepts which we consider basic axes of thought, both for the "architects" of the monasteries which concern us and for Aalto, regarding creativity in architecture. Concerning the issue of harmony, nature, in both cases, functions as a standard of inspiration for the propose architecture[108], in spite of the fact that the influence of nature is

---

[107] Fisher house, Hatboro, Pennsylvania (1960); Eleanor Donnelly Students' Residence, Bryn Mawr, Pennsylvania (1960-1965); First Unitarian Church, Rochester, New York (1959-1967); Dominican Convent (project), Media, Pennsylvania (1965-1968); Library and Refectory, Exeter, New Hampshire (1967-72); Indian Institute of Management (1962-74); Sher-e Bangla Nagar, Dhaka, Bangladesh (1962-83); Salk Institute for Biological Studies, La Jolla, California (1959-65).

[108] G. Schildt, *Alvar Aalto*, p. 219.

different, in order for harmony to be complete (for Aalto it comes from the shape of the Finnish forests, while in Greek monasteries, from the shape of mountains). It is clear that in the work of Aalto, the idea of harmony in the organic adjustment of architecture to the virgin environment is pure and strong, in any building program, to the point that Goran Schildt, when he analyzes the setting of the buildings of the Finnish architect, compares them to the Byzantine monasteries of Mount Athos.[109]

The concept of harmony, of course, does not refer only to architecture, but also reflects the deeper idea of harmony in mankind. Aalto tried to adjust the life of the human community to the course of nature, by starting from the psychological concept of man.[110] This effort coincides with the spirit that Christian coenobitic monastic life proposed since early Christian times. The movement of the soul is a reality in human life, whether it is deep and intense or superficial and light. This composite situation appears to be known in monastic life, which confronts it immediately, and in fact we could say that its architectural expression follows this realism harmoniously, without deceit.

The source of the cultural heritage in both the monastery complex and the work of Aalto is completely different. The Orthodox monastic coenobite culture and the architecture which represents it originate from the early Christian tradition of the Holy Fathers and from Byzantine civilization. For Aalto, however, the origin is the tradition and the architecture of Karelia.[111] In spite of their differences, there are points of contact between the two architectural expressions, namely the following:
- Both are flexible in terms of their development. They start from a small cell and develop into an open structure,

---

[109] A. Aalto, *Works I*, p. 16.
[110] G. Schildt, *op. cit.*, p. 218, B. Zevi, *Spazi*, pp. 353-375.
[111] G. Schildt, *op. cit.*, p. 229. K. Frampton, *op. cit.*, p. 176.

like a biological group of cells from which an entire complex is formed.[112]
- In terms of construction, both are expressed with the materials of their site, a fact which allows the expression of a more local evolution of architecture.
- In both, the construction is functional, plastic-organic, and expressively flexible, that is, we observe a romantic-contextual architecture, which comes from human activity and is expressed as a flexible container.[113]

In both cases, without following strict architectural dogmatism, it is always taken into account that the only dogma is to follow the rules of nature, which are more natural; thus, with their architecture, a national romanticism is created.

Romantic architecture is characterized by the variety and multiplicity of its elements, and in fact it is not easy for us to understand *"logically"*, because it seems illogical and subjective, as it shows an intense *"expression"* in its shape and appears as an addition, rather than something organized. The atmosphere and the expressive character of this romantic architecture, for both the Greek monasteries and Aalto, is found in the midst of a composite total form[114], which is completed with various elements and would agree with Venturi's theory that *"both-and"* is better than *"either-or."*[115]

We could also characterize both types of architecture as *"topological"*, since they desire to adjust the structure of the building space to a specific setting. In this way, topological forms which are built with the natural materials of the area are introduced[116]. In this architecture, we note that:

a) The building is not simply a container, but is an expressive and active presence in the environment,

---

[112] G. Schildt, *op. cit.*, p. 229.
[113] V. Scully, *Modern Architecture*, pp. 39-40.
[114] C. Norberg Schulz, *Genius Loci*, pp. 69, 195.
[115] R. Venturi, *Complexity*, p. 23.
[116] C. Norberg Schulz, *Meaning*, p. 213.

b) Its composition includes elements from the past and tradition, and

c) The concepts of freedom and order appear together in the design, as basic characteristics.[117]

All these characteristics make up the particularity of each building and their pluralistic nature.[118]

Anyway, it is also significant to say that the pluralist architecture of both the Greek Byzantine and post-Byzantine monasteries and the architecture of Aalto coincide in their starting point, that is, the fundamental issue of the architectural program. This idea is based on the concept of *"hierarchy"*, which is implemented with the independent form of the dominant element of the building program, which is emphasized and complemented by some changes in materials and construction. In monastic architecture, this concept is understood in terms of the building of the *Katholikon*, the main church of the monastery, while in the work of Alvar Aalto, it is found in the council hall of the town halls[119], in the Auditorium of the theatre or cultural centers[120] or in the reading room of libraries.[121]

Another issue which emphasizes similarity in the comparison between Aalto and Greek monastic architecture is the presence of a collage-like design. Collage is meant with the sense of the art

---

[117] This freedom does not mean or favor permissiveness, caprice, or arbitrariness, but it means that the architectural solution is free to be formed by itself as the product of internal and external forces. C. Norberg Schulz, *op. cit.*, p. 219.

[118] C. Norberg Schulz, *op. cit.*, p. 219.

[119] Saynatsalo (1950-52), Seinajoki (1963-65), and Alajarvi (1967-69). A. Aalto, *Works I*, pp. 137-145, 230-235, A. Aalto, *Works II*, p. 54, and K. Fleig, *A. Aalto*, pp. 147, 153, 155.

[120] Helsinki Kultuuritalo (1955-58); Wolsburg Cultural Centre (1959-1962); Helsinki Concert and Convention Hall (1967-71).

[121] Seinajoki (1963-65); Rovaniemi (1965-68); Mount Angel Benedictine College, Oregon, U.S.A. (1967-70).

and sprit of the Cubism of Picasso and Braque[122], which allows the merging of contradictory elements and the use of various shapes and materials, creating a dynamic play of opposites in the façades of buildings, like a painted collage. In Aalto's work, the graphic imagery[123] of modern architecture is combined with the anonymous Finnish tradition. In monastic architecture, on the other hand, the Byzantine graphic imagery is merged with the anonymous Greek tradition of construction. In other words, we could describe the application of various architectural motifs and shapes, which is proposed by such a synthetic structure, as *"polyphonic."*[124] We consider *"polyphonic"* the solution of the morphological architectural problem in which, in the entire structure, some geometric regularities are in play at the same time as a dynamic three-dimensional plasticity, without excessive repetitions and symmetries. The richness of this architectural design is sought through the deviation from rectangular combinations and the continuous movement in the general image of the building (plan, cross-section, and views) and emphasized with the variety of textures, multiple rhythms and articulations, and materials. All these elements form together, synthetically, the idea of architectural *polyphony*.

In this play of contrasts, it is worthwhile to mention briefly the concepts that Porphyrios[125] defines concerning the way in which Aalto designed and thought: *heterotopia*, *discriminatio*, and *convenientia*. We observe these concepts in the architectural composition of Greek monasteries. *Heterotopia* refers to the overturning of the continuity of composition, and consists of a unity of fragments coming from different sources. *Discriminatio*, which belongs to the activity of the mind, where ideas are not planned strictly according to predetermined categories, but are researched and differences are defined, forms the adjustment of a basic type (*typos*) to the particularities of a place (*topos*); in other

---

[122] J. Pallasmaa, *A. Aalto's architecture*, p. 409.
[123] J. Pallasmasa, *op. cit.*, p. 409
[124] J. Pallasmaa, *op. cit.*, pp. 412-413
[125] D. Porphyrios, *Eclecticism*, pp. 2-3.

words, type is sacrificed in favor of place. The third concept originates from this: the *convenientia* in the adjacency of the various morphological elements which are articulated and implemented further, out of different materials, according to the convenience of functionality and the availability of materials and technology.

At this point it is worthwhile to consider some unanswered questions related to the comparison which we make here between Greek monastery architecture and the work of Aalto, because while we observe that their manner of material implementation and era differ, their treatment of the general problem of architecture and their solutions, in general, are similar.

- Is this the most correct and sincere expression of architecture and good architects who are sensitive to people, their activity, and the environment where they live?
- Do good architects, wherever they are located, respond with the same *"logic"*, namely, with responsibility, respect, and at the same time, with sensitivity and creativity, with the thought that man reacts psychologically in a similar fashion everywhere, when it is a question of his habitat?

In both monastery buildings and Aalto's work[126], the style of life is taken into account in the architectural proposition. The Site plan is affected by the particularities of the place, and in the end, the architectural type gives a separate *"identity"* to the buildings, while simultaneously solving its functional requirements. Lifestyle, setting, and architectural type mark an architecture which covers human desires and needs, is harmonized with the natural environment, and possesses intense plasticity, thus composing what Le Corbusier claimed about architecture:

"Architecture is the wise, correct, magnificent interplay of volumes under light..."[127]

---

[126] S. Groak, *Aalto's Approach*, p. 112.
[127] Le Corbusier, *Vers une Architecture*, p. 178.

As we approach Le Corbusier's thoughts in terms of architecture, this permits us to distinguish some forms of expression which coincide with the way that Byzantine and post-Byzantine monasteries took shape in Greece. Although this took place in an almost empirical manner, we discover today that some stages of the creative research of the Franco-Swiss architect, both in his written work and in his architectural practice, would theoretically support the composition of the Greek Orthodox monasteries.

From Le Corbusier's "research" we selected three routes of expression which we also meet in Greek monastic architecture.

a) The idea of the integrated work of art (*Gesämtkunstwerk*).

Le Corbusier, as a writer, resurrects the idea of the *Gesämtkunstwerk* at a very early stage (1921-1925), expressing the change of life with a new spirit that would cover architecture, urban planning, industrial design, and painting.[128] From another side, monastic life, which essentially proposes a conversion of human life to the renewal of the heart and spirit, supported by the Holy Scripture[129], proves the idea of the *Gesämtkunstwerk* in the following way: it takes on architectural form with the monastery, which is characterized as a *miniature city*, as we will see below, which is complemented by the standardized "design" of items of daily use and by iconography. We could say that the design of these items (glasses, plates, bottles, etc.) which are used at the monastery's tables, which always had a simple design with clear shapes, expressing the simplified harmony that covers basic

---

[128] Charles Jencks, *Le Corbusier and the Tragic View of Architecture*, pp. 61-62. Le Corbusier wrote four books (*Vers une architecture, Urbanisme, L' Art décoratif d'aujourd' hui*, and, with Ozenfant, *La Peinture Moderne*) in which his articles in the magazine *L' Esprit Nouveau* are republished; in these, he explains the complete change in modern life through the *Gesämtkunstwerk*.

[129] Psalm 50(51):12, Colossians 3:10, Ephesians 4:20-24.

needs (food and drink), was a "lesson" from the monasteries of Mount Athos for Le Corbusier.[130] A similar design of items of daily life is also found, with industrial means, in the evolution of the ideas of Bauhaus (1919-32).

The iconography of Orthodox churches and monasteries follows the Christian pedagogical tradition dating from Early Christian times. This is a substantial type of pictorial expression, which through a broad program, attempts to make the eschatological reality of the Kingdom of God felt within the functional space.[131]

In the iconographic plan, nothing is casual concerning the placement of images. Instead, it is connected with the architectural shape of the church and the hierarchy of the space where the images are depicted.[132] The voluntary, symbolic, and complete decoration of the church, where all the walls from the atrium and narthex to the sanctuary (*ierón*) resemble being *"covered with brocade"*, in Le Corbusier's description from when he visited Mount Athos[133]; this is not, of course, an expression of *horroris vacuum* (fear of empty space), but a depiction of the environment of the Kingdom of Heaven.[134] This art, that of mural painting, together with the musical art of Byzantine chant, creates an unrepeatable religious climate and an atmosphere of pious prayer.[135] In this manner, a complete and

---

[130] Jencks, *op. cit.*, pp. 32-33.

[131] In the *katholikon* (main church) of the monastery, a miniature of the "City of God", the most important themes depicted are Christ Pantokrator in the dome, a symbol of the heavens, the cycle of the main celebrations of the year, figure of prophets, martyrs, and ascetics. G. Matthew, *Byzantine Aesthetics*, pp. 95-96; Charles Delvoye, *Byzantine Art*, vol. A, pp. 14-15,106, 176 and vol. B, pp. 269-287; M. Siotos, *Holy Images*, pp. 158-172.

[132] P.A. Michelis, *Esthétique de l' art byzantin*, pp. 142-145.

[133] Giuliano Gresleri, *Le Corbusier viaggio in Oriente*, pp. 283-284.

[134] M. Kalligas, *The Aesthetics of the Space*, pp. 55-57, and D. Pallas, *The Aesthetic Ideas*, pp. 313-331.

[135] C. Cavarnos, *Byzantine Sacred Art*, pp. 87-88.

integrated Christian monastic work of art is complemented, one which characterizes one era and civilization: the Byzantine.

b) The *"brutalist"* expression.[136]

Early in his career, Le Corbusier understood that architecture with unrefined materials could result in emotive relationships. In his architectural practice, during the 1930's, he communicates in some of his work, mainly houses[137], with the language of the local dialect, expressing the sincerity of unrefined materials. This expression forms a basic principle of *"brutalistic"* architecture[138] and a significant construction type which we find in the Greek Orthodox monasteries of the Byzantine and post-Byzantine periods, as an expression of the age and subject (fortress and monastery architecture). In this way, this architecture acquires the identity with which it is recognized in history. Le Corbusier, after the Second World War, although he does not completely follow this current, will return to *"brutalistic"* expression with the construction of some residences.[139] This is an architecture which orients itself to the expressive power of the form of the

---

[136] B. Zevi, *Spazi dell' architettura moderna*, p. 613. "...*In 1955, R. Banham expresses the concept of the new brutalist current: topology rather than geometry, use of unrefined materials and an unprejudiced roughness of architectural language, expressed with the materials and the type of construction...*"

[137] House of Mr. Errázuriz in Chile (1930), Le Corbusier – P. Jeanneret, *Oeuvre 2*, pp. 48-52. Weekend house in the suburbs of Paris (1935); Mathes House (Ocean) (1935), Le Corbusier – P. Jeanneret, *Oeuvre 3*, pp. 124-130, 134-139; Jaoul House (1937), Le Corbusier, *Oeuvre 4*, p. 12.

[138] Frampton, *op. cit.*, p. 238.

[139] "Roq" and "Rob" at Cap Martin (Mediterranean) (1949), re-interpretation of the weekend house in Paris (1935) in the form of a residential prototype: Le Corbusier, *Oeuvre 5*, pp. 54-61. Jaoul house at Neuilly-sur-Seine (1952/1953), proposal by Le Corbusier, *op. cit.*, pp. 173-77, and construction (1954/56): Le Corbusier, *Oeuvre 6*, pp. 208-221. Sarabhai House at Ahmedabad (1955/56), Le Corbusier, *op. cit.*, pp. 114-131.

traditional house, and turns itself in part toward the style of unrefined, natural materials. Today, a return to the authenticity of Byzantine construction is also necessary for a proper renovation of monastery buildings, without being bothered by the speed of time, which in the particular case of monasticism never had any meaning. In contrast, thanks to the philosophy of time found in the formation of monasteries, the monuments that testify to an eternal architectural culture factually identified with the substance of monastic life reach our age.

c) A plastic, organic, and dynamic design: *Notre-Dame du Haut-Ronchamp*[140].

In this pilgrimage chapel, Le Corbusier proves his sensitivity to man, his activity, and in fact to the space which will receive them, applying in this way the metaphysical thought of Heidegger, which hints that architecture is useful for symbolizing the existence of man in space.[141] The plastic *"mass"* of Ronchamp, the expressive structure of its completely white wall with its empty spaces being small windows, the interior idea of a cave, and the character of a sculpture in the isolated setting are the most important elements which emphasize the influence of Cycladic architecture on Le Corbusier, and reminds us of the monastery of Hozoviotissa in Amorgos. This monastery, like all Byzantine and post-Byzantine monastic architecture in Greece, offers with its buildings the meaning of religious architecture, which Le Corbusier stated at Ronchamp "...*as a vessel for intense concentration and thinking*..."[142] Thus, since Byzantine time, the monastery formed, as a building, a mystical space in order to cover the essence of the need of the human soul, which

---

[140] The Chapel of Notre Dame of Haut de Ronchamp (1950-54), Le Corbusier, *Oeuvre 5*, pp. 72-84, and Le Corbusier, *Oeuvre 6*, pp. 16-39. L. Hervé, *Le Corbusier, l' artiste l' écrivain*, Neuchatel, 1970, pp. 20, 25-26, 34-35.

[141] Martin Heidegger, *Poetry*, pp. 158-159.

[142] Le Corbusier, *Oeuvre 5*, p. 72.

in monasticism specifically is the *"thirst of the soul for God."*[143] Le Corbusier understood this need, and for this reason he constructed a corresponding building (form and space), Notre Dame du Haut-Ronchamp, and named it *"ineffable space."*[144] From this parallel and its result, we reach the following question: did this mysticism which is presented in Notre Dame du Haut-Ronchamp result from Le Corbusier's memories of the monastic landscape of Mount Athos? This question appears because of a physical comparison between Ronchamp and Frank Lloyd Wright's proposal for a Greek Orthodox church in the United States (closer to our topic), where the result, in spite of all the genius and sensitivity of the master of Taliesin, is not so successful.

However, in Wright's houses and words we find some themes that were expressed in Greek Byzantine and post-Byzantine architecture, as is proven, for instance, by the compact and solemn nature of the mass of the houses designed by Wright, where an articulated, continuous and fluid space is enclosed.[145] The above constitute a central concept of plasticity as an element of continuity of space in Wright's philosophy of design.[146] The essence of this idea evolved in the compact Byzantine monasteries, which contain an internal articulated and flowing outdoor space as a *"container."* These spaces, both in Wright's work and in the monasteries that concern us, provide a clear expression of dynamism and unity from the elements that structure them, while simultaneously offering protection as a closed space, in the sense of a shelter. The elements that articulate these internal spaces are set at the center, and form reference points ("landmarks" in architectural discourse) for the traditions to which they respond. That is, they contain

---

[143] Psalm 41(42):3
[144] Le Corbusier, *Oeuvre 6*, p. 16. *"espace indicible"*: *"the plastic event which is characterized as ineffable space: the appreciation of dimensions is erased before the inconceivable..."*
[145] V. Scully, *Modern Architecture*, p. 21.
[146] V. Scully, *Frank Lloyd Wright*, pp. 17-18, and Frank Lloyd Wright, *An Autobiography*, pp. 139-150.

architectural and symbolic meaning. In Wright's houses, this landmark is the fireplace, while for monasteries it is the *katholikon* (main church). Just as the *katholikon* is considered the heart of the monastery, in Wright's houses the fireplace[147] constitutes the heart of the dwelling.[148] Each one, in its own built environment, forms the most significant point of welcome and warm meeting. For Wright, the fireplace is the place for true fire[149] and this element symbolizes the forces and order of nature;[150] that is why is located at the center. At this point man can test or live out the meaning of freedom and participation, dealing with the basic meaning of his existence.[151]

Thus we discover that Orthodox monastic architecture, in the Byzantine and post-Byzantine periods and continuing until today, expressed similar ideas of participation and freedom, in a way (the common prayer of the coenobites) and in a special space, the *katholikon* (the monastery church), in which, under its dome, the might and order of the Pantokrator are gathered symbolically.[152]

Returning to the concept of the shelter, in the two cases that we are comparing, one may observe that both follow the human being as measure of the entire building design. The meaning of this issue, we could say, is that for the human being, the building tries to be on his own scale, and consequently to be felt his personal place.[153] The idea of shelter, expressed on a human scale, is a basic element in Wright's proposals for houses, because the shelter offers to the psychological dimension of man coverage, protection, safety, and an atmosphere for him to be

---

[147] The fireplace or the hearth, which was always considered the gathering point for the family. For this reason, we never find two fireplaces in traditional houses.
[148] C. Norberg Schulz, *Genius Loci*, p. 192.
[149] "...*The fire burning deep in the solid masonry of the house...*" Frank Lloyd Wright, *Natural House*, p. 37.
[150] C. Norberg Schulz, *Meaning*, p. 182.
[151] C. Norberg Schulz, *Genius Loci*, p. 194.
[152] II Peter 1:16-21
[153] Frank Lloyd Wright, *op. cit.*, pp. 32-33.

with himself and his family.[154] Coenobite monasticism, which contains a family character, symbolizes the retreat of man to God[155], and is applied in the Orthodox monastery at a human scale, in order to offer to the whole brotherhood and the monk individually an appropriate refuge for total devotion to God.

The result of the architectural implementation of Wright's houses, which are set in places outside the city center and are characterized by an integral design, as happens with human integrity, comes from two basic united thoughts cultivated during his life: *individual freedom* and *hunger for reality*.[156] In this way, we could accept that it is no coincidence that Orthodox monasticism, which is characterized as individual, chose remote places in order to face freely the hunger for reality of spiritual life, constructing an integral building that will cover it: *the monastery*, which solves the problem or issue of dwelling, as it belongs to the earth, but looks towards the heavens.[157]

Concerning the study of the types of Frank Lloyd Wright's houses, the Prairie (1890-1916)[158] and the Usonian (1937-1947)[159], we can say that his types evolved according to a course similar to that of monastery types in Greece. From a basic exemplary building, a central idea starts out and is tested, based on which a flexible variety of organization, floor plans, and various architectural shapes (volumetric elements) are developed.

---

[154] E. Kaufmann – B. Raeburn, *Frank Lloyd Wright*, pp. 42, 317, 319.
[155] Psalms 17(18):3, 56(57):2, Proverbs 14:26.
[156] Wright, *op. cit.*, p. 13.
[157] "...in the essential nature of the dwelling, on the ground also means under the sky..." Heidegger, *op. cit.*, p. 13.
[158] Wright, *Work*, pp. 56-59. D. Martin house, Buffalo, New York (1904), pp. 45-53; E. Martin house, Oak Park, Illinois (1907), pp. 72-75; Robie house, Chicago, Illinois 91908), pp. 112-115; Robert house, River Forest, Illinois (1908), pp. 66-68; Gale house, Oak Park, Illinois (1909), p. 64.
[159] J. Sergeant, *Wright's Houses*, pp. 17-18; Goetsch-Winkler house, Lansing, Michigan (1939), pp. 54-55; Lloyd Lewis house, Libertyville, Illinois (1940), pp. 66-67; Pew house, Madison, Wisconsin (1940), pp. 68-69.

For Wright, this was the Willits house, and in monastic architecture, it was the monastery of Saint Catherine of Sinai.

Another issue which characterizes Wright's work is the search for a course from the entrance to the hierarchical area of the building. We can discover a similar concept developed in Byzantine monastic architecture. This is a transitional course through space, which comes about when, from the narrow, low, and half-dark entrance, we reach the central internal outdoor space, which is open and lighted, causing surprise with the difference in light, height, and breadth of space.

Three other concepts that determine and complete the course of design and the architectural means of expression of Frank Lloyd Wright were also dominant in the design of Greek Byzantine monastery architecture, where they developed, unified, in a similar and authentic way. They are the following: *organic architecture*, *integrity*, and *the nature of materials*.

a) In Frank Lloyd Wright's view, *organic architecture* consists of a manner of design which originates from the ground, and is not just a solution based on aesthetics and love of fashion, but a movement toward the deep idea of integrated human existence, where art, religion, and science constitute a unity of *form and function*.[160] The basic and inevitable theme in organic architecture, which is proven in the architecture of Greek monasteries, is the kinship between the building and the soil. The beauty of harmony is brought about in a natural and elementary kind of integration and integrity. The concept of integration in organic architecture is expressed in the ideology of Frank Lloyd Wright, and coincides metaphorically with the deep internal search of the monk for his integration with his Creator through spiritual life.

---

[160] Wright, *Organic Architecture*, p. 47.

b) *Integrity*[161], according to Wright, is needed in both architecture and the human being, and in fact, he sustains that it must be a substantial, deeper virtue of the building.

"...*In speaking of integrity in architecture, I mean much the same thing that you would mean were you speaking of an individual. Integrity is not something to be put on and taken off like a garment. Integrity is a quality within and of the man himself. So it is in a building. It cannot be changed by any other person either, nor by the exterior pressures of any outward circumstances; integrity cannot change except from within because it is that in you which is you... To build a man or building from within is always difficult to do because deeper is not so easy as shallow...*"[162]

With this definition, we could say that both monasticism and monastic architecture were the result of a similar mentality, where from a different concept of freedom, another concept of life arises, a spiritual one, which in an architectural sense constitutes a natural and integral rendition in the environment, in the specific setting and in the lives of the inhabitants, the monks.

c) *The nature of materials*[163] forms a part of the philosophy of Frank Lloyd Wright's design, which tried to complete the naturalness of *organic architecture* and its *integrity*. His thought starts out from the analysis of the strength of an endless treasure, the earth. The earth is the rich natural source of all materials, but their working is in the hands of the architect, in order for us to have an authentic architectural result. On his *"palette"* the materials will be used according to their structural characteristics of plasticity, hardness, porous texture, and in fact, they will appropriately determine the mass, proportions, outline, shape,

---

[161] Wright, *Natural House*, pp. 121-123.
[162] Kaufmann – Raeburn, *op. cit.*, p. 293.
[163] Wright, *op. cit.*, pp. 52-53, and Kaufmann – Raeburn, *op. cit.*, pp. 222-224.

and color of the building. In this way, architecture will have a character and a natural tone that will emphasize organic architecture and its integrity unanimously. Such a *"syntax"* of architecture regarding materials and their peculiarities was written, in terms of buildings, in a natural way in the Byzantine and post-Byzantine eras with their churches and monasteries. The basic vocabulary of this architecture was stone, brick, and wood, materials used according to their natural constructive and aesthetic virtues. Monastery architecture in Greece has expressive character and its own identity, thanks to these materials and their use in the manner of construction.

From the above it results that in *"anonymous"*[164] Byzantine and post-Byzantine monastery architecture in Greece, there has been an application of principles that we find in the concerns of modern *"creators"*, in the rationalist architecture of Le Corbusier and Louis Kahn, and also in the organic architecture of Frank Lloyd Wright and Alvar Aalto. In the table below, these correlations become clearer:

---

[164] C. Conenna, *Monastic Architecture*, chapter 3.3.1 "Tradition and Monastery Architecture."

Nature	Human	Building
Place	Way of life	Architecture
Natural Environment	Common life	Monastery

To conclude, it deserves to be noted that the concern about architecture that tries to serve, with a building, a human way of life, in a specific place, was made real in Byzantine monastery architecture, putting into effect buildings with the language and syntax of space, function, technology, and form, and producing various concepts and ideas which later (in the 20th century), without our sustaining that there was some influence transmitted, would make up separate currents of architectural ideology, represented by the masters of the first and second generations of modern architecture in various countries of the Western world.

Chapter 4

Monastery Architecture and Residential Organization

The organization of monastery complexes and residential organization of a city show similarities. Just as cities have monuments, spaces in between, residential and service buildings and all these elements coexist in harmony for the purpose of serving people better, thus, monastery complexes also have similar elements for the function of the coenobite community.

However, residential organization is not simply a gathering of residents, but something additional, a society. Similarly, the community of coenobite monks is something more than a simple brotherhood or a group of monks; it is a monastic community with a common spiritual purpose.

The internal outdoor monastery area (whether in the Western or the Eastern monastery), just like the square of a settlement, function as a place of gathering. We may say that both resemble a man-made oasis for the human soul. Monks in the internal outdoor monastery space and the residents of a settlement in the square escape from the pace of daily labor. In this way, we approach the theory of Anastasios Orlandos, who describes Byzantine monastery architecture as «*a miniature city*».[165]

The rendering of the «*urban*» character of Greek monastic architecture in the Byzantine and post-Byzantine ages, as it took form during the centuries and reached our time, can be emphasized through three theories of recognized modern architects: C. Sitte, K. Lynch, and G. Cullen. Each of these theories contributes to research into Greek monasteries because it contributes to the analysis of their architectural composition and their organization, and in fact they help us to understand better the qualitative concepts that are found within monastery architecture. The theory of C. Sitte aids the study of the «*monastery space*», that of K. Lynch aids the interpretation of the «*monastic place*», and finally, the theory of G. Cullen aids the understanding of the «*Monasticscape*».

The specific selection of these three theoretical works, out of a significant part of the range of great theoretical architects and urban planners, is due to the observation that their views aid in an

---

[165] A. Orlandos, *Monastery Architecture*, pp. 7-12.

approach to the particularities and characteristics of Greek monasteries. We observe that these theories are very close to the way that we see monastery architecture, and by extension they help document our views. Approaches through these analyses shed light on structural elements that usually escape the notice of only historical and archeological studies.

The common point of all three of these theories is that they all give a special weight to the human factor and human psychology. They observe human behavior and reactions within the urban environment, extending their conclusions from the scale of urban planning to that of architecture.

C. Sitte, with his criticism of the «*artificial*» mechanical conception of cities (that is, proposals designed on a drawing board), tried to support the «*organic*» evolution of the urban environment, and followed a «*natural model*».[166] In addition, C. Sitte did not attach special importance to the form of the container, but to the quality of the contained element: space.[167] The «*anonymous*» Greek monastic architecture of the Byzantine and post-Byzantine ages displays a variety of improvisations in internal outdoor areas, which present aesthetic values similar to those of the squares of medieval towns that C. Sitte studied.

Two later architects from the '50's, K. Lynch in the United States and G. Cullen in Great Britain, analyzed the design of public areas of the urban environment, providing us with two different approaches:

- The former appears more rationalistic and defines five elements, as we have seen above (*paths, edges, nodes, landmarks and districts*)[168] in order to render the image of the urban environment. These five elements, according to Lynch, help people to orient themselves within the urban web, a fact which

---

[166] «Natural model» = transformations of design that go beyond the architecture of the drawing board. D. Gostling – B. Maitland, *Concepts*, pp. 25-26.
[167] S. Kostof, *City Shaped*, p. 84.
[168] K. Lynch, *The Image of the City*, p. 46.

provides them with psychological security. With this perception of his, Lynch offers us an important «*Theory of Place*»[169], which we find in Greek monasteries and use to interpret the «*Monastic Place*».

- The latter is more romantic and creates a «*visual glossary*» in order to complete another view of the urban environment and make the principles of urban planning more understandable. His analysis is based on «*serial vision*» of the urban environment. In this way, he reveals to us a different side of the topic, «*the visual quality of the environment*»[170]. Cullen concentrates his attention on the different perceptions of the elements of the urban environment, according to the course that each observer follows through it,[171] defining in this way the concept of the «*Townscape*». We adopt these ideas of Cullen's in order to explain the «*Monasticscape*» of the Greek monastery complexes of the Byzantine and post-Byzantine period.

The *Monastic Space* and Sitte's Theory (1843-1903)

C. Sitte, in his work *City Planning according to Artistic Principles* (1889), praises the shape of medieval towns as an example to be imitated. Sitte was against the rationalistic style of modern life and believed that in earlier times people knew the «*art*» of living together as a society, a fact which resulted in the creation of the environment that we admire today.

The wealth of Sitte's research is due to the meaning that he gives to settlements that have an irregular (non-geometric or non-rational) shape of squares that also provoke the observer's interest. In his research on the design of medieval squares in Italy and Germany, he put forward the view that the square, as a common outdoor area, constituted the appropriate way for a

---

[169] C. Norberg Schulz, *Genius Loci*, New York 1984, p. 20.
[170] E. De Mare, *G. Cullen*, p. 84.
[171] D. Gostling – B. Maitland, *op. cit.*, p. 153.

unifying settlement system including public and private buildings to be created.

«...*Aristotle also required just this of a city plan -that temples to the gods and other civic buildings should be united in a suitable way- while Pausanias declares in this connection that one could not use the term 'city' for something lacking public buildings and plazas...*»[172]

In his book *City Planning according to Artistic Principles* (1889), Sitte tries to find the aesthetic elements of old medieval squares. He analyzes the beauty of spontaneity in architectural composition, as well as design by intuition, which contrasts with severe geometric plans.

Among other things, Sitte studies the following:

- The relationship that there should be among buildings, monuments, and their plazas.
- The view that squares should be independent entities with an enclosed spatial character.
    - The irregular shape of medieval plazas.
    - Groups of Italian squares.

We may say that Byzantine monasteries, mainly those on a large scale, are like a miniature ancient or medieval walled town[173], with common buildings, temples and squares, organized according to coenobite monastic principles. By extension, in the monasteries that are not the product of a specific architectural study, we consider that somehow we identify Sitte's theory of medieval settlements that are formed with irregularly shaped squares. These squares do not have geometric form, nor axes of symmetry, but nevertheless they have harmony and are picturesque.

At this point it deserves mention that although the scale of Sitte's examples is different (*urban planning*) from that of

---

[172] C. Sitte, *City Planning*, p. 8.
[173] A. Orlandos, *op. cit.*, p. 7.

monasteries (*architecture*), the same main idea of the space's organization is followed.

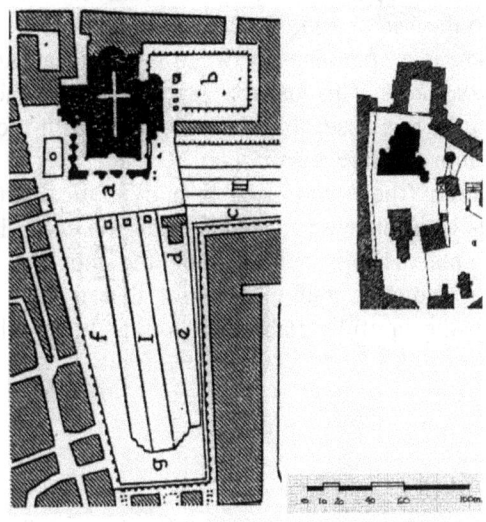

**Piazza San Marco- Venezia /
Monastery Vatopediou Agion Oros**

In the architectural composition of enclosed Greek monasteries, Sitte's idea of settlement finds its application. In these monasteries, there is the *katholikon* as an architectural monument, around which the enclosed outdoor area is developed.

The distance from the *katholikon* to the wings varies, and consequently affects the forms of the squares or outdoor monastery spaces. We could see this proportion as a ratio of «full» to «empty» («*full*» = built, «*empty*» = internal outdoor monastery space).

We observe three tendencies in this «full» to «empty» ratio:

1. The internal outdoor space «*dominates*» over the monument. This usually takes place in large-scale enclosed monasteries, since the internal outdoor space occupies a much greater expanse compared to the *katholikon*.

2. The monument «*dominates*» the internal outdoor space. This usually takes place in small-scale monasteries, since the internal outdoor space occupies a relatively small expanse compared to the *katholikon*.

3. There is a «*balance*» between the internal outdoor space and the *katholikon*. This usually takes place in medium-sized monasteries. In this case, the dimensions of both the *katholikon* and the outdoor area are «*harmonized*».

The church (the *katholikon*) is a dynamic element, which with both its location and its shape, affects the entire image of the monastery area. This is achieved by the fact that the church «*defines*» the squares and vice versa, that is, the squares are improved by the carefully elaborated architecture of the church.

The *Monastic Place* and Lynch's Theory (1918-1984)[174]

Monastery Dochiariou – Agion Oros

Christian Norberg Schulz, in his book *Genius Loci: towards a Phenomenology of Architecture*, uses the concept of the «man-made place»[175], in which he distinguishes two categories for analysis: space and its character. Space is manifested by the three-dimensional organization of the elements that form the place, and character, by its «*atmosphere*».

In our case, the monastery is a building that consists of a shell protecting the monks, and becomes understood within the

---

[174] K. Lynch, *City Dense*, pp. 9-23.
[175] C. Norberg Schulz, *op. cit.*, p. 50.

three-dimensional organization of its own place. The *monastic place*, however, is the monastery as a building, with a specific spiritual character, its «*religious atmosphere*». That is, it is the «overall» expression that comprises the building and the life that it acquires during its use.

The «enlivening» of the place is supported by Lynch's theory[176], which analyzes the way in which «*identification*»[177] of man with the place occurs. This identification begins with «*orientation*»[178] and is completed with the «*imageability*» or «*visibility*» of architectural elements.

Lynch, with the concepts of «*visibility*», the «*legible*», and «*imageability*», defines the physical quality of the architectural object, that is, form, color, location: elements that help the process of identification and the creation of mental images.[179]

Monasteries are easily «*legible*», as centers of spiritual and religious activity. Architecturally, the enclosed shape and the fortress-like form of a monastery complex reinforces the introspection of coenobite monastic life, a characteristic that is interpreted as the «*monastic place*».

The distinct image that the observer or user has of the monastery results initially from its distinction from remaining buildings: in other words, from its architectural «*identity*». Secondly, this idea is influenced by the practical and emotional value that it has for every observer.[180]

The "*Monasticscape*" and Cullen's Theory (1914-1994)[181]
Cullen's work, *Townscape*, is the art of architectural relationships.[182] It is art that «*ties together*» the «*messiness*» of buildings, streets, and public spaces forming the urban environment, making it have visual coherence. As with Sitte,

---

[176] K. Lynch, *Image*, p. 46.
[177] K. Lynch, *op. cit.*, p. 8.
[178] K. Lynch, *op. cit.*, pp. 129-131.
[179] K. Lynch, *op. cit.*, p. 9.
[180] K. Lynch, *City Dense*, pp. 97-99, 104-111.
[181] E. DeMare, *op. cit.*, pp. 81-85.
[182] S. Kostof, *op. cit.*, p. 91.

Cullen as well is opposed to the architecture of the grid and strict geometric volumetry in the planning of modern cities.

In *Townscape* (1961), his study of the urban setting, Cullen defines concepts, some of which could find their best depiction in Greek monastic architecture as well. The English architect speaks of the art of the «*man-made environment*» based on spontaneous aesthetic principles and tries to preserve, through sketches and photographs, cases of urban areas where these principles were applied.

By studying Cullen's concerns for the urban setting or «*townscape*», we may say briefly that Cullen analyzes it as «spaces, surfaces, and punctuation points». His analysis forms an evolution of Sitte's theory of outdoor public spaces. More specifically, while the subject of Sitte's study is outdoor public spaces (mainly squares) as independent «*elements*», Cullen studies outdoor public spaces in relation to other factors that influence their image (such as surrounding buildings, the formation of green space, etc.). This exact differentiation is the center around which the entire theory of the «*townscape*» is developed. We adopt the concepts that Cullen uses in order to study the «*monasticscape*». More specifically, these concepts are the following:

Concerning outdoor space	Concerning the surfaces of views	Concerning punctuation points
Enclosed – closed	Projections	Contrast
Squares – narrows	Niches	Symbolic Point
Intimacy – Mysticism / Mystery	Continuity	Metaphor
Deflections – Succession of spaces	Incident	

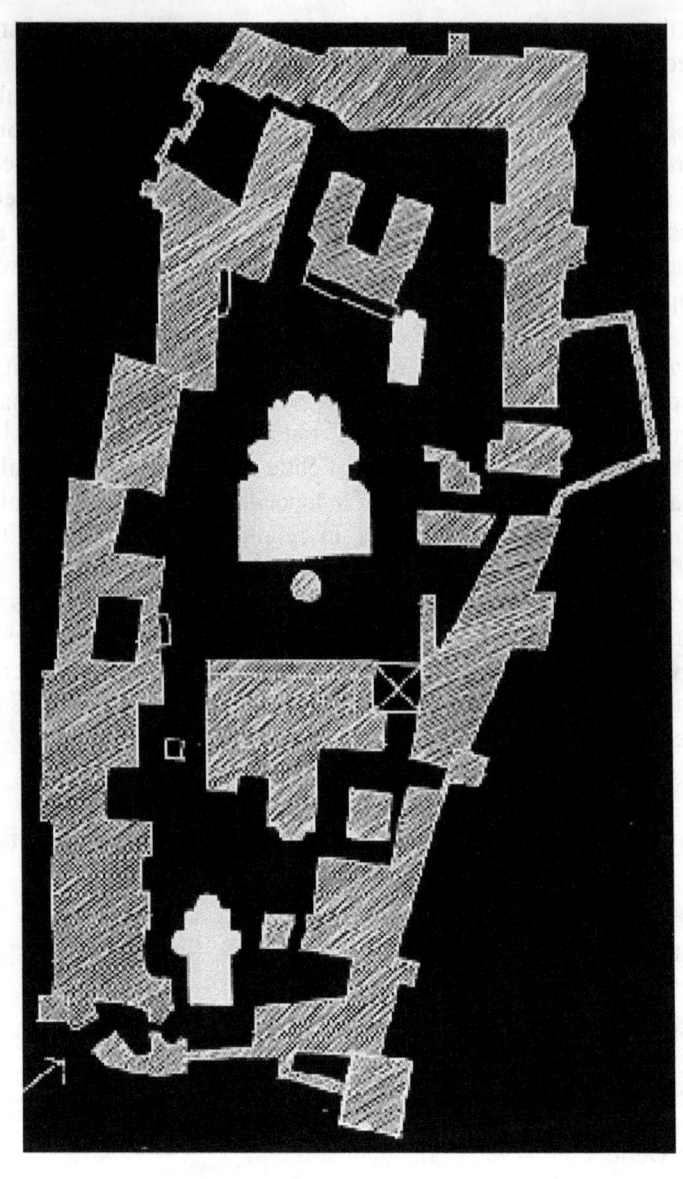

Monastery Megisti Lavra – Agion Oros

In Further Detail:
Enclosed outdoor space (enclosure)[183] and closed outdoor space (closure)[184]

Enclosed outdoor space (enclosure) has various forms and corresponds to the enclosed and semi-enclosed architectural type of Greek monasteries. The idea of enclosure also appears in the monastery complexes of the west, in the form of a cloister. Another difference existing between internal outdoor areas of Christian monasteries in the West and East is that in Eastern monasteries and especially Greek ones, the enclosure is not a unified «pure» space, but some buildings are inserted within it, such as the *katholikon*, the *phiali*, and the *refectory*. In some way, these buildings divide the enclosure into smaller internal outdoor spaces. These spaces are places for gathering and communication for the monks and visitors.

Closed internal outdoor space (closure) is «*dynamic space*», that is, a space that causes movement (walking, etc.). Closure usually has a linear form. Closure may consist of a path or passage. We find such types of internal outdoor spaces in Greek monasteries of the linear architectural type with outdoor or semi-outdoor space.

Both categories of internal outdoor space, enclosure and closure, emphasize the introversion that is pursued in Greek monastery architecture.

---

[183] G. Cullen, *Townscape*, pp. 25, 27, 29, 30, 32, 33, 35-52, 97-102, 137-8, 162-3, 177, 179, 182-7.
[184] G. Cullen, *op. cit.*, pp. 30, 45, 47, 106-10, 137-8.

Monastery Koutloumousiou - Agion Oros

Deflection[185], Narrows[186], and Succession of Spaces[187]

The «*deflection*» of a building differentiates it from the remaining buildings and provokes the observer's curiosity. The «*deflection*» of a building is its rotation around a new axis, a different one from the axis of the road that is followed by the remaining buildings.

The «*narrows*» are openings created in the space by «*contractions*» between the buildings. These narrow passages connect the internal outdoor spaces. This results in a «*succession of spaces*» and a «*space fluctuation*». (Flowing changes in the dimensions of the internal outdoor spaces).

The dynamic nature of the internal «*Monasticscape*» is reinforced by the «*deflections*» and the «narrows» created because of the setting of the *katholikon* and at times those of the *refectory*, the *phiali* and the bell tower. In addition, the plasticity of volumes and the formation of the views of the wings contribute to this effect. Just as for Cullen, a town is not a pattern of streets but a succession of spaces[188], thus, the monastery's internal outdoor space constitutes a succession of corresponding intermediate spaces.

---

[185] G. Cullen, *op. cit.*, pp. 43, 108, 187.
[186] G. Cullen, *op. cit.*, pp. 43, 45, 109, 120.
[187] G. Cullen, *op. cit.*, pp. 17-20, 46, 55, 106-10.
[188] G. Cullen, *op. cit.*, p. 46.

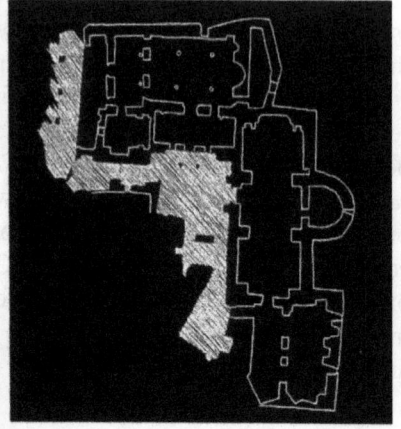

Monatery Ag. Ioannis Theologos – Patmos

Intimacy[189] and Mystery[190]

As we have already mentioned, the monastic *«place»* is interpreted from the form of the building and its character. In the character of Byzantine and post-Byzantine monasteries, the sensation of *«possession»*[191] of the land by the monastery is very intense. This *«land domination»* in Greek monastery complexes becomes more perceptible in the enclosed outdoor monastery space. The *«monastic place»* and the *«monasticscape»* are characterized by *«intimacy»* and *«mystery»*. Both of these concepts reflect the spirit of monastic life. However, we observe that they are more intense in enclosed monastery complexes on a small scale, where the internal outdoor spaces are more «compressed».

Monastery Panagia Aimialón-Gortynia

---

[189] G. Cullen, *op. cit.*, pp. 69, 177-9.
[190] G. Cullen, *op. cit.*, p. 51.
[191] G. Cullen, *op. cit.*, p. 21.

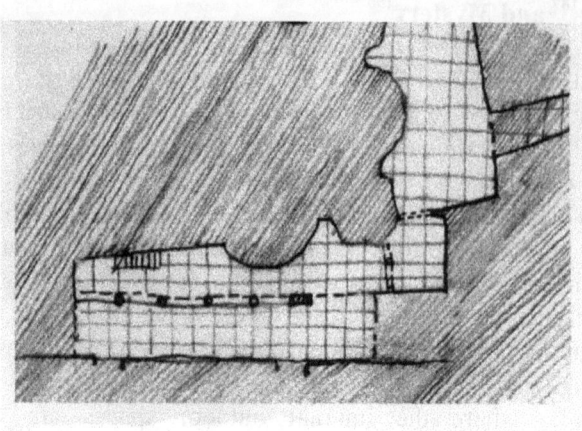

Monastery Dionysiou – Agion Oros

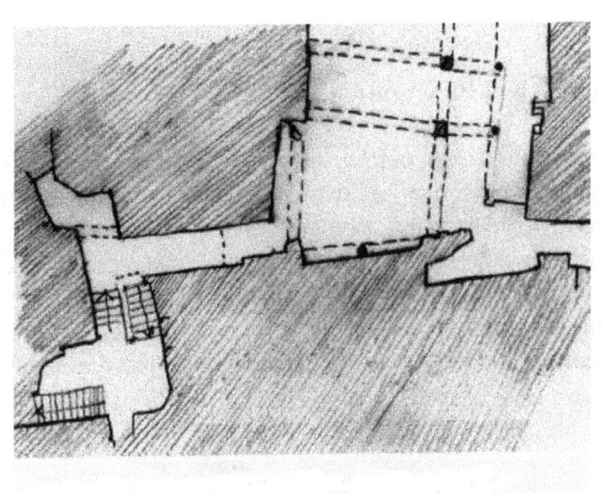

Monastery Ag. Ioannis Theologos - Patmos

Incident[192] and Punctuation[193]

«*Incident*» and «*punctuation*» are two concepts that we adopt in architecture in order to express «*pauses*». An architectural «*pause*» may be any element that interrupts a continuous morphological architectural rhythm. An «*incident*» is an element that creates a «*pause*» in the continuous rhythm of the views of a building. A «*punctuation*» is a morphological or volumetric architectural element that creates a «*pause*» in the development of space.

Monastery Xenofontos – Agion Oros

«Incidents» in the monastic architecture examined are the *sachnisiá*[194], the balconies, the *liakotá*[195], etc. on the walls

---

[192] G. Cullen, *op. cit.*, p. 44.
[193] G. Cullen, *op. cit.*, pp. 26, 30, 35, 45.
[194] Sachnisiá = gr. Σαχνισιά plural of Sachnisí= enclosed wooden volumetric projection of an upper floor or part of it supported by diagonal beams.
[195] Liakotá = gr. Λιακωτά plural of Liakotó = Room enclosed in glass and exposed to the sun.

surrounding the monastery. The *katholikon*, the bell tower, and the *phiali* can be considered «*punctuation*», since they are «architectural objects» that «interrupt» the monastery space and «interfere» in pedestrians' routes. The «*punctuation*» often also has a depictive nature that makes them be like sculptures within space.

Monastery Megisti Lavra – Agion Oros

We could say that the «*incidents*» and «*punctuation*» are the details that play the determining role in the formation of the «*monasticscape*». The existence of many «incidents» results in a dynamic interplay of projections and recesses.

Continuity[196]

In the internal Byzantine «*monasticscape*» we observe a «*continuity*» in the view of the wings. By the concept of continuity, we mean the lack of «*interruption*» in the overall image of the views by the addition or the modification of a morphological element; in other words, we mean the lack of «*pauses*» as they were defined above. More specifically, we have «*continuity*» in Byzantine monasteries in the view of the gallery, which is located in front of the cells of the monks, which are placed in a row.[197] There was also continuity in the walls of the Byzantine monasteries. However, after the additions to the upper section of the wall which took place during the late post-Byzantine period, «*pauses*» were created. Nonetheless, the «*continuity*» was maintained in the lower section of the walls, a phenomenon that we could define as «*sectional continuity*».

Monastery Koutloumousiou – Agion Oros

---

[196] G. Cullen, *op. cit.*, pp. 55, 184.
[197] A. Orlandos, *op. cit.*, p. 32.

Monastery Ag. Bissariona - Trikala

Chapter 5

The Monastery and its Symbolism

The monastery, in architectural terms, is a specific phenomenon that includes buildings, facilities, structural elements and a characteristic arrangement of volumes. It is a living reality of the material side of cenobite monasticism. On the other hand, as long as the monastery is considered an architectural construction, this means that it refers to more than a construction that was built to cover the monks' practical needs. In particular, it concerns the human psychological and spiritual existence, which is expressed in architecture and finds meaning in the expression of space and in symbolic forms. The viewpoint of the historian and architect Christian Norberg Schulz contributes particularly to the understanding of these properties of monastery architecture: this view considers architecture *"the concretization of existential space"*, emphasizing in this way the importance of human existence, meaning, and symbolism in architecture.[198]

Another interesting view concerning symbolism in architecture is that of the Spanish historian and architect F. Chueca Goitia, who sustains that architecture is the art of the symbolic form, because it expresses from the finest and most human things, to the most composite and vast. He also emphasizes that art constitutes, since time immemorial, the most important contribution and the best morphological expression of the culture of a people, in its efforts to express all that is collective, historic, traditional, and even at the highest level, divine[199], as also occurs in the case of the spiritual life of monasticism. With this rationale, we can understand the importance the Spanish historian gives to the role of architecture, by which symbolism is supported.

The Byzantine monastery, as a religious building and especially as a spiritual institution, is implemented architecturally according to a functional organization based on Christian faith and by extension, the morphological result may be interpreted symbolically. This symbolism refers to the placement of the

---

[198] Christian Norberg Schulz, *Meaning*, pp. 221-223; Norberg Schulz, *Existence*, pp. 17-33; Norberg Schulz, *Intentions*, pp. 62-64.

[199] F. Chueca Goitia, *Arquitectura Española*, p. 22.

elements of the architectural program, to the proportions and form of volumes, the use of materials, and simple unadorned forms. The founders usually used local materials in the construction of the monastery (stonework, brickwork, and wooden structures), which "spoke" architecturally with sincerity, as in primitive architecture.[200] This is a sincerity that the monk is supposed to seek and is transferred to his architecture. The form and typology of the most basic elements of the monastery's plan vary, according to the space available in the monastery and its setting in the natural environment, which often imposes a specific architectural plan for the monastery.

The main characteristics of a monastery, as an architectural object, are its location in an isolated place, and its introverted form. We could say that these characteristics acquired a base in the early Christian community, when monasticism was established and founded itself on basic teachings of Christ, such as, for example, self-denial[201] and secret prayer.[202]

The structure of the monastery symbolically reflects the Christ-centered nature of coenobitic monastic life, which has remained unaltered for more than 1000 years in Greece, and more than 1500 in the Christian East. The architecture of these buildings becomes symbolic for the Orthodox faith, and seals the identity of Eastern Christian and Greek monasticism. Both the architecture of the monasteries and the iconography which decorates it create a devout atmosphere which helps the monks in their spiritual task of prayer. Christ, who is the cornerstone of his

---

[200] R. H. Hitchcock, *Frank Lloyd Wright*, p. 56.
[201] "... I say to you, that if the seed of grain does not die after falling on the ground, it alone remains. But if it dies, it brings much fruit. The one who loves his soul will lose it, and the one who hates his soul in this world, will keep it in eternal life. If anyone serves me, let him follow me, and wherever I am, my servant will also be there. If anyone serves me, the Father will honor him." John 12:24-26.
[202] "But when you pray, go into your room, close your door, and pray to your Father in secret, and your Father, seeing you in secret, will reward you visibly..." Matthew 6:6-7.

church[203], based it on the central idea of contact with God through prayer of the heart:

> "...the prayer of the mind, of Evagrios, in the East becomes the 'prayer of the heart', a personal prayer, which is clearly addressed to the Word made flesh, 'the prayer of Christ', where the remembrance of the Name occupies a central position..."[204]

We understand the symbolism which is mainly reflected individually in the places of worship and spiritual use of the monastery's plan in the following manner:

The *Katholikon*:

In the *katholikon*, (the church of the monastery), the monk and the believer seek and find the presence of the Lord, and this, we would say, is the reason why the *katholikon* is completely differentiated in architectural terms from the remaining buildings of the monastery complex and is placed at the center. It has a general geometric plan which originates from a very composite architectural synthesis of pure symbolic forms and shapes: the cross, the rectangle, the cube, the circle, and the dome.[205] This symbolism is completed, in some cases, by the use of visible brick, or by pigmented surfaces, painted an intense red (as some

---

[203] Matthew 21:42 "... the stone rejected by the builders became the head of the corner..."

[204] J. Meyendorf, *St. Gregory Palamas*, p. 40.

[205] G. Prokopiou, *Secular Symbolism*, pp. 99-133. "The rectangle (the Earth with the four spirits: the winds), the cube (the world), the dome (the heavens, where the Almighty is found0, the cross: the cruciform shape of the ground plan (redeeming love, Christ, the Messiah, the Savior, the Word, the second person of the Trinity, the history of Jesus on Earth), the circle and the dome [symbolize] the heavens, or the semi-circular vault located towards the east [symbolizes] Paradise..." Also A. Guillou, *Civilisation*, pp. 378-382.

katholika of Mount Athos). In Christianity, the church is a symbol of the heavenly Jerusalem.[206]

Katholikon Monastery Megisti Lavra - Agion Oros

Therefore, there is no monastery without a church: that would be illogical and certainly meaningless. The space of the *katholikon*, with its internal architectural articulation, the interplay of light and shadow, the "decoration" with the didactic arrangement iconography, the iconostasis, and all the elements which aid the church's function, prove how essential its space is

---

[206] G. Prokopiou, *op. cit.*, p. 186, and A. Lagopoulos, *Religious Symbolism*, pp. 65-67.

for the life of the building, just as the Holy Spirit is for the Christian.[207]

---

[207] The symbolism of this idea is documented in the Holy Scripture: see Romans 8:1-17.

The Refectory:

In this space, where the monks dine following the principles of protocol (*typikón*), the relationship among the abbot and the monks becomes more perceptible. Every meal resembles Christ's Last Supper with the Disciples. We could say that also, with the presence of the refectory, the existence of the brotherhood as an eschatological community living simply, as regards worldly items, is made real. The symbolic message of the refectory is made understandable through the brief duration and austerity of the meal, in an atmosphere of silence, where only one voice is heard, that of the reader of the word of God.

Refectory Monastery Dochiariou – Agion Oros

The *Fiali*:

With this sculptural-architectural element, the holy sacrament of baptism is symbolized, the visitation of the Holy Spirit, the symbol of new life. Besides, monastic life is essentially a new life offered exclusively to God. In terms of shape, the *fiali* resembles a small area for baptizing (a baptistery). Its dome is painted on the inside with images of the holy sacrament of the baptism of Jesus Christ and other events from the Old Testament related to baptism, the prophetic announcements of this holy sacrament, and the reception of the Holy Spirit, as it is expressed in the scriptures.[208]

A symbolic reason why we would say that the *fiali* is centripetal and centrifugal in its architectural organization is the following: being centripetal emphasizes introversion, symbolizing self-knowledge, and being centrifugal means extroversion, symbolizing love for one's neighbor, two practices exercised in monasticism.

We could also suppose that if the *fiali* existed in all monasteries, the three spaces of the monastery, the *katholikon*, the *refectory*, and the *fiali*, "would depict" the Holy Trinity: the Father, the Son, and the Holy Spirit receiving their respective architectural form in the *katholikon*, the *refectory*, and the *fiali*. In the oldest and most important monasteries of Mount Athos, these buildings are located along an axis which also "inscribes" the fundamental principle of Christian faith, the Holy Trinity.

---

[208] See Matthew 28:19-20, 4:13-17, Ephesians 4:5-6, Romans 6:3-9, John 1:26-28, 1:31-34, 7:37-39.

Fiali Megisti Lavra - Agion Oros

The Bell Tower:

This symbolizes the "calling", the "invitation". This invites the monks and pilgrims to the processions, and in essence, to prayer. The sound of the bell or the gong, as well as the rhythm and volume of this sound, remind every monk of his own personal merits, with which his life can be used to the advantage of good, and he can help his fellow men properly.

Bell-Towers

Monastery Vatopediou- Agion Oros

Monastery Ag. Ioannis Prodromos- Serres

Thus, we understand the symbolism which the monastery contains overall as a spiritual institution and an architectural construction as follows:

- **The monastery as a spiritual institution**:

Monasticism, as a mentality and a way of life, is based on the teaching of the perfection of man. Man and the whole of creation have lost their original, natural destination and are in the unnatural situation of fall, which, however, is reaching its end. Light and truth will dominate with the coming of the Kingdom of God.[209] Monks distance themselves from worldly things not out of hatred for the world, but out of desire to live under the conditions of the will of God, in whose image and emulation they were created.[210] Thus, poverty, chastity, and obedience are not simply three virtues which the monk tries to acquire, but three basic preconditions for the spirituality which aims at the eschatological perfection of human nature. The *hesychastic* method of prayer, with the concept of "return to oneself" (silence)[211], aims at the sight of the divine light and the *theosis* of human nature.[212] However, the asceticism of the monks *in Christ*

---

[209] "The night has left, and the day arrived..." Romans 13:12.
[210] Genesis 1:26-27, 5:1, 9:6.
[211] J. Meyendorff, *St. Gregory Palamas*, p. 138. Concerning the spiritual character of silence, see Matthew 6:18, Ephesians 1:11-19. The proverbs of monks concerning the value of silence are also characteristic: "Whoever has learned to be silent finds rest everywhere.... An abbot says that if you acquire the virtue of silence, do not boast that you have achieved something important. Rather, convince yourself that you are not worthy even to speak..." (The Abbot Poimen), T. Hambakis, *Gerontiko*, pp. 239-240.
[212] Concerning the spiritual meaning of light in the New Testament, se Matthew 5:13-16 and 6:22-24, John 1:8-9 and 8:12. In the spirituality of Orthodox monasticism, light obtained a fundamental importance: "When the prayer of Christ is turned into a prayer of the heart, its first result is enlightenment..." see J. Serr, *Filocalia*, p. 15.

does not remain a personal matter for them, but through liturgical life and the cenobite way of life it maintains a clear ecclesiastic nature. The monk aims not only for his personal sanctification, but he is also responsible for the final return of creation to its Creator.[213] The architecture of monasteries tries to express and to give precision to these perceptions, and not simply to create places for housing the monks as it might understand.

- **The monastery as a work of architecture:**

This is the space that *"houses"* the spiritual concerns of the monks, while offering them physical safety at the same time. The *katholikon* is the spiritual refuge of the monks, and the defensive tower protects them from incursions. The fortress tower is the "eye" of the monastery towards the outside. We can say that the defensive tower and the walls towards which the cells are oriented make up a building unit. A similar unit is made up by the *katholikon* and the bell tower. The former protects the monks physically, while the other protects their soul and spirit. Observing the arrangement of enclosed monasteries, we could say that the fortress of the monastery *"embraces"* the fortress of the soul.

The internal outdoor area of the monastery, which can be characterized as its *"soul"*, appears dynamic, with various shapes, and is never unitary. In fact, we could say symbolically that movement within it is like the movement of the soul of the monk in his spiritual life toward salvation and eternal life.

---

[213] I. Zizioulas, *Creation*, pp. 118-119.

Monastery Simonos Petra – Agion Oros

With these concepts and their symbolic parallels, we can consider that there is a symbolic correlation between the buildings of a monastery complex and the human organism. This correlation corresponds to modern architectural theories related to the human organism or biology. The first which we observe is Hugo Haring's[214] theory of *organhaft*[215], in which buildings are "organs" for the functions that they serve, as are the organs of our body. A second theory expresses the thoughts of Peter Collins[216] on architecture as a "biological organism", in which a biological structure can be applied to the architectural organization of a building. Related to such a concern is the biological parallelism that leads us to the separation of functions or organs, according to Le Corbusier:

"...*The plan sets organs in an order, and thus an organism is created. Biology: a great word for architecture and urban planning.*"[217]

In a similar way, Alvar Aalto[218] considers biology a source of inspiration for architecture, and notes that

"...*biology has rich and abundant forms with the same construction, the same tissues, and the same principles of*

---

[214] C. Norberg Schulz, *Genius Loci*, p. 71, and *Meaning*, p. 203.

[215] *Organhaf* should not be confused with the concept of the "organic". The organs (the elements of the architectural plan) organically form a whole, where every element has its own function and correspondingly its own form, as well as its own placement within the whole. Another perception of organic architecture, as we will see below, it the way in which a building adjusts itself organically (in terms of shape, following the plasticity of nature) in the morphological variety of a specific environment.

[216] Peter Collins, *Biological Analogy*, pp. 303-306, and *Modern Architecture*, pp. 149-158.

[217] Le Corbusier, *City*, pp. 147, 231, 269, and C. Jencks, *Le Corbusier*, p. 123.

[218] G. Schildt, *Alvar Aalto*, p. 221.

cellular organization, and it can create billions of combinations, where each one of these depicts a perfect and evolved shape..."

From this point of view it is sustained that the things which surround man are cells and tissues, living beings like him. And he continues,

"...as architectural components supplement human life, they must be harmonized with the human dimension..."

Another thought on the same topic is that of the Greek cultural anthropologist G. Megas[219], who speaks of "organic evolution" in his research on traditional architecture in Greece. Evolution which is created by the variety of forms, which display coherence and interdependence.

Based on the above thoughts and approaches, we may sustain that there is the following correlation among the parts of the monastery's space and the parts of the human body:

The monastery	+	the internal outdoor area	+	the katholikon	+	the katholikon's interior
↕		↕		↕		↕
The body	+	the soul	+	the heart	+	the spirit

---

[219] G. Megas, *Popular Construction*, p. 4.

Monastery Karakalou – Agion Oros

The thought of this correlation coincides with the interpretation of some texts[220] on the mystic life of Byzantine *Hesychasm*.[221]

Thus, the Eastern Orthodox monasteries and especially the Greek ones are organized, in most architectural types, with the *katholikon* at the center of the coenobitic complex, as the "*heart*" of the monastery. The pure geometric shape of the *katholikon*, as a symbol of perfection, comes into contrast with the unregulated form of the monastery's remaining buildings. It is as though Christ himself were symbolically located at the center of the monastery.

Perfection and imperfection are expressed in the following ways:

---

[220] "... the body, soul, and spirit were considered as a single organism. Only sin rotted this unity, leading to an uprising of the body against the spirit, surrendering the spirit to imagined adventures, and enslaving the body to the tyranny of passions. Christ came to restore human harmony, and the hesychast, with the fixed memory of the Name of Christ, makes redeeming grace dwell deep within himself. In order for this grace to become truly effective, it is necessary for the *hesychast* to '*bring the spirit back into the heart*,' that is, to give it the place that belonged to it, at the center of the organism of body and soul, and to restore thus the harmony among the various parts that compose it... (Pseudo-Macarius)", J. Meyendorff, *op. cit.*, pp. 73-74. Pseudo-Macarius also sustains elsewhere that "...*the heart is the part that dominates and possesses leadership of the body, and inside it, the Creator placed the source of internal warmth*...", J. Meyendorff, *op. cit.*, p. 73.

[221] Byzantine hesychasm of the 13th and 14th centuries is footed in the tradition of the Greek fathers and the ancient church, and completes the mystic tradition of Macarius (390), Evagrios (399), and pseudo-Macarius (473), who had oriented the mystic life of hesychasm in the direction of a unitary organism of body, soul, and spirit. J. Meyendorff, *op. cit.*, p. 133.

a) Science determines that Euclidean geometry is an expression of the perfection of shapes[222], while irregular (non-Euclidean) geometry is an expression of imperfection.

b) Christian faith sets Christ as an example of perfection, and the better a Christian is, the more he will approach the perfection of God.

In order to express and reinforce the symbolic significance of the *katholikon* relative to the remaining buildings of the monastery complex, we can make a parallel with an excerpt from the Holy Scripture:

"...*We hold this treasure in earthen vessels*..." (II Corinthians 4:7-8).

Therefore, we humans are vessels of clay with our heart as a valuable treasure, and the human body is considered a receptacle for divine grace, just as the Son of God himself was incarnated in the womb of Mary. A similar phenomenon takes place in the architecture of monasteries. The *katholikon*, expression of perfection, is the "treasure" found inside the "*earthen vessel*", the surrounding buildings which give form to the wings of the monastery, an expression of imperfection.

In this sense, we can hold that in monastery architecture, human language (art[223]) communicates with and meets the language of God (nature).[224]

Besides the religious symbolism contained in Byzantine and post-Byzantine architecture, it is important to note briefly the characteristics of design that make it interesting today.

---

[222] E. Papanoutsos, *Logos*, p. 124, and H. Papoutsopoulos, *Pascal*, p. 13.

[223] V. Scully, *Louis Kahn*, p. 36, and R. Giurgola – J. Metha, *Louis Kahn*, p. 34.

[224] J. Serr, *op. cit.*, p. 25.

The founders applied architectural solutions for the monks' buildings in a simple and natural way, empirically, we could say, with a free creative spirit, as was their faith. They constructed building with the materials that nature gave them in the place where they were located, with multiform organic shapes, in harmony with the setting of their asceticism, and in their own measure. They preferred closed shapes in order to aid concentration, asceticism, and protection. The final architectural result covered their monastic spiritual desire for silence and intimacy.

In further detail, we observe that in the ground plans of Greek Byzantine and post-Byzantine monasteries, beyond their organization by type[225], these are buildings that attach great importance to their setting. They attach themselves to the setting harmoniously, to the point that the architectural type is sacrificed. Therefore, the result in the ground plan is a flexible, organic, articulated but also always functional organization. In addition, the topography of the setting itself is many times so varied that it favors a diversified cross-section, which creates rich spatiality, that is, it provokes an interplay of various levels, with courts, balconies, squares, stoas, etc. This varied cross-section, combined with the architectural scale of monastery buildings, which is always at the human scale, could be said to provide the concept of a refuge.

Concerning the topic of the composition of monastery views, we could point out that with the passing of time, it constituted a composite design of dynamic composition, merging shapes, materials, and colors. Some order is always observed in the composition, where the relation between shape and background appears clearly. The internal views of the monastery's wings, that is, those of the internal outdoor space, present a "dug" background, because in general, they consist of continuous stoas. Externally, the background is compact, because it consists of a fortress wall that encloses the monastery.

---

[225] C. Conenna, *Monastic Architecture*, Chapter 2.2.2: *"Typology of Greek Monasteries"* p.178.

The plastic organization of the ground plan, the varied cross-section, and the articulated views (both the open internal view and the closed external one) create the following aspects in monastery architecture:

Internally, within the outdoor monastery area, a dynamic, fluid, and simultaneously united space is created.

Externally, however, a compact, many-shaped, and expressive three-dimensional plasticity is created as the overall volumetric result.

Monastery Ag. Ioannis Prodromos – Serres

Conclusion

Beyond the theological religious symbolism that emanates from this architecture, it is important to note summarily the characteristics of design that make it still interesting in our days as an architectural fact. The builders applied architectural solutions for the monastery buildings in a simple and natural way, we could say, even an empirical one, with a free and creative spirit, as their faith was as well. They built monasteries with the materials that nature gave them in the place where they were located, developing varied organic schemes in harmony with the place of asceticism and on its scale. They preferred closed shapes in order to help them with their concentration, monastic asceticism, and protection from any invasions they might have to face. We observe, however, that the Byzantine and post-Byzantine monasteries of Greece, in the entire range of their typology of spatial organization, possess flexible and articulated floor plans, although they always have a clear functional scheme.

The dynamics of topography itself consequently, in architectural terms, favor a varied cross-section, creating a rich, interesting, and mysterious character of the space of the building, causing a polysemic interplay of levels among the patios, galleries, small squares, terraces, and staircases, with the inclusion in certain cases of trees and grass, interwoven with stone floors, usually made of smooth stone. We find innumerable spaces with these characteristics and their most varied combinations within this anonymous monastic architecture, an aspect that, naturally, provides it with a stamp of individuality.

Consequently, the Byzantine and post-Byzantine monasteries of Greece may be considered works of architecture with solutions for many issues of architectural design, which are known to be inherent concerns for the creative architects of our age.

Within the translation of the theological into the architectural, we deal with a few details as unavoidable particularities that show us the transcendence of the philosophical and theological in the development of monastic architecture. We will not say that the builders of these monasteries used Holy Scripture as a manual for building, since it is known that they kept it as a source of wisdom in the spirit by which they lived.

In architectural terms, this type of human experience with deep spiritual content, which surpasses the eminently rational and logical, caused the production of a free and varied type of architecture, adapting itself to the dynamic characteristics of the physical context, without imposing itself on it as a foreign and dominant object. It allows for a high level of particularity in the development of the main structural ideas of the monasteries, which are only repeated in terms of typology, allowing the formal and volumetric part of the architectural fact to accommodate themselves organically and contextually to nature, with the aim of not being transformed into architecture that follows a model. The resulting effect is an architecture based on *figure* more than *form*. We could say that it is a localized architecture with a heterogeneous formal response in which variety prevails over order, without reaching disorder or chaos, and where the specific and the concrete prevail over the general and the abstract. Avoiding monotony, it presents itself as figurative, localized, and regional, beyond the systematic, purposeful, and international.

Finally, we conclude that both Byzantine church architecture and that of the monasteries, explorative and creative in all their levels of expression, placement, the functional, spatial, formal, constructive, and depictive – can still be a source of inspiration, since it still transmits lessons of design to us. We only need to exercise our sight in order for their discovery to extend to other generations.

Photographic Credits,

Prolegomenon
Monastery Ag. Pavlo- Agion Oros (Painting Edward Lear 1858):
A. Paléologue 1997 Le Mont Athos, merveille du christianisme byzantain, p. 128.

Chapter 1
Katholikon Monastery Dochiariou: Hellier Ch. 1997 Greek Monasteries, Athens, (Greek version), p. 162
Drawing plan of Katholikon Monastery Megisti Lavra, Agion Oros: Alpago Novello, 1969 Grecia Bizantina, Milano, p. 102

Chapter 5
Monastery Simonos Petra – Agion Oros and Monastery Karakalou – Agion Oros: Athos from the Heavens, Heli Photo, Athens.

Bibliography

Sacred Scriptures

La Biblia, ed. Paulinas, R. Ricciardi y B. Hurault, Madrid, 1974.
Biblia de Jerusalén, ed. Desclée de Brouwer - Bilbao, 1975.
Antiguo Testamento
Septuaginta, ed. A. Ralhfs, Stuttgart, 1965.
Nuevo Testamento
The Greek New Testament, ed. By K. Aland, M. Black, G. M. Martini, B. M. Merzger, A. Wikgren, 1975.

General Bibliography

Aalto A. 1970 Complete works -band I (1922-1962), Zurich
Aalto A. 1971 Complete works -band II (1963-1970), Zurich
Allchin A.M.1971 Man as image and mystery, Athens, (Greek version).
Alpago Novello, 1969 Grecia Bizantina, Milano
Argan G. C. 1963/12 *«On the Typology of Architecture»* Architectural Design.
Argan G. C. 1984 Tipologia I *«Tipologia»* Coleccion Summarios 79, Buenos Aires
Bouras Ch. 1994, "*The Byzantine Tradition of Ecclesiastic Architecture in the Balkans during XVI and XVII centuries*". The Byzantine tradition after the fall of Constantinople, Athens, (Greek version).
Braunfels W. 1972 Monasteries of Western Europe, the architecture of the orders ed. Thames and Hudson ltd. London
Brownlee D./ De Long D. 1991 Louis I. Kahn in the realm of architecture, Los Angeles, New York
Cavarnos C. 1957 Byzantine sacred art, New York
Ching F. 1982.Arquitectura, forma, espacio y orden. Ediciones G. Gili S.A. - Mexico D.F.

Christou P.K. 1991, "Ecclesiastic Literature, Fathers and Theologians of the Christianity", Volume 2, Thessaloniki, (Greek version).
Chueca Goitia F. 1947. Invariantes castizos de la architectura espanola. Madrid - Buenos Aires
Collins P. 1959/754 A. R. *«Biological analogy»*
Colquhoun A. 1981 Essays in architectural criticism, New York
Conenna C., 1999, Monastic Architecture in Greece, Space and Symbolism, PhD. Polytechnic School, Aristotle University of Thessaloniki, Thessaloniki, (Greek version).
Cullen G. 1961 The concise Townscape, London
Deligianni Dori E., 1993 Survival of Byzantines and new forms of Post-Byzantine architecture, Athens (Greek version).
Delvoye Ch.1983 Byzantine Art, Volume 1-2 Athens, (Greek version) (trans. M. Papadaki),.
De Mare E. AR 10/1996 «Gordon Cullen» p. 81-85
De Wolfe I. AR 6/1962 «Italian Townscape» p. 383-444
Fleig K. 1975 Alvar Aalto, London
Frampton K. 1987 Modern Architecture, History and Critic, Athens, (Greek version)
Giurgola R. and Metha J. 1989 Louis I. Kahn architect, Barcelona
Gostling D. & B. Maithand 1984 Concepts at urban design, London - New York
Gresleri G. 1984 Le Corbusier viaggio in Oriente, Venezia - Paris
Groák S. 1993 *«Aalto's approach to movement and circulation»*. Companion to contemporary architectural thought, London - New York
Guillou A. 1963 *«Grecs d'Italie du Sud et de Sicile au Moyen age I: Les moines»* Melanges d'archeologie et d' historie - Paris
Guillou A. 1974 La civilisation byzantine, Paris
Hambakis T. 1993 Gerontiko, Thessaloniki, (Greek version).
Hancock, John E. "On the Greekness of Greek Architecture", Orion volume in honor of Professor D.A. Fatouros,

volume A, Academic Bulletin of the Polytechnic School of the University of Thessaloniki, Department of Architecture, vol. XV, Thessaloniki, 1998,

Heidegger M.1971 Poetry, language, thought (translation and introduction Albert Hofstadter) New York

Hellier Ch. 1997 Greek Monasteries, Athens, (Greek version)

Hitchcock R.H. 1942 In the Nature of Materials. The buildings of Frank Lloyd Wright (1887-1941), New York

Hilberseimer L. 1955 The Nature of Cities. Paul Theobald & Co. Chicago

Jencks Ch.1973 Le Corbusier and the tragic view of architecture, Harvard university press - Cambridge Massachusetts

Kahn L. 1974/5 A. D. *«Credo»*

Kalligas M., 1946 The Aesthetics of Space in the Greek Church during Medieval period, Athens, (Greek version).

Kambouri Vamvoukou Maria, 1993 "*Church Architecture in Macedonian after the fall of* Constantinople *(1453-1912)*", Macedonia Archaeology and Culture, Volume 2, Athens, (Greek version).

Kaufmann E. and B. Raeburn. 1974. Frank Lloyd Wright writings and buildings. New American Library times mirror, New York, London, and Scarborough Ontario.

Kostof S. 1991 The City shaped. Urban patterns and meanings through history. «organic» patterns, London

Kyriakidou-Nestoros A. 1977 Theory of the Greek folklore (critical analysis), Thessaloniki, (Greek version)

Lagopoulos A. 1997 The Byzantine city, "the religious symbolism of the Byzantine city, Archeology and Arts, Athens (Greek version)

Le Caisne M. - Bouillot J. 1978 El paisaje ser o no ser *«Sitio y entorno»* Coleccion Summarios 25/26 Buenos Aires

Le Corbusier et P. Jeanneret 1957 Œuvre Complete 1929-34 Vol. 2 ed. Girsberger- Zurich

Le Corbusier et P. Jeanneret 1964 Œuvre Complete 1934-38 Vol. 3 ed. Girsberger- Zurich

Le Corbusier 1955 Œuvre Complete 1938-46 Vol. 4 ed. Girsberger- Zurich
Le Corbusier 1966 Œuvre Complete 1946-52 Vol. 5 ed. Girsberger- Zurich
Le Corbusier 1958 Œuvre Complete 1952-57 Vol. 6 ed. Girsberger- Zurich
Le Corbusier 1965 Œuvre Complete 1957-65 Vol. 7 ed. Girsberger- Zurich
Le Corbusier 1958 Vers une Architecture. Ed. Vincent Freal & Co. Paris
Le Corbusier 1967 The Radiant City, London
Le Goff J.1972 La civilisation de l'Occident Medieval. Ed. Arthaud – Paris
Lobell J. 1979 Between silence and light, spirit in the architecture of Louis I. Kahn, Colorado
Loos A. 1972 Sämtliche Schriften μτφρ. L.Cirlot/P. Perez: «Ornamento y delito y otros ensayos», Barcelona
Lynch K. 1972 The image of the city. The MIT Press - Massachusetts
Lynch K. 1990 City dense and City design writings and projects of Kevin Lynch The MIT Press Cambridge, Massachusetts and London.
Mango C. 1974 Arquitectura Bizantina. Ediciones Aguilar - Madrid
Mathew G. 1963 Byzantine aesthetics, London
Matsoukas N. 1998 History of Byzantine Philosophy, Thessaloniki, (Greek version)
Mc Carter 1994 Fallingwater - Frank Lloyd Wright, London
Megas G. 1969 Objectives and Methods for the research of Popular Construction, Athens (Greek version)
Meyendorff J. 1974 A study of Gregory Palamas ed. The faith press 2nd ed. Great Britain (translated from the French by G. Lawrence «Introduction a l'etude de Gregorie Palamas»
Meyendorff J. 1989 Saint Gregory Palamas and the Orthodox tradition, Athens, (Greek version).

Meyendorff J. 1974 The Byzantine Hesychasm, Athens, (Greek version).
Michelis P. A. 1959 Esthétique de l'art byzantin. Ed. Flammmarion - Paris
Michelis P. A. 1965 Aesthetic Theorems, Volume 2, Athens, (Greek version).
Moutsopoulos N.K. 1956 The Architecture of Churches and Monasteries in Gortynias, Library of Archeological Etairias Athens #38, Athens, (Greek version)
Moutsopoulos N.K, 1979 Ano Poli -Thessaloniki, morphological and building details, Thessaloniki.
Mylonas P. 1964, The Architecture of Agion Oros, Nea Estia, Athens, (Greek version)
Norberg Schulz Ch.1968 Intentions in Architecture. M.I.T. Press - Cambridge, Massachusetts
Norberg Chulz Ch. 1971 Existence, Space and Architecture, New York
Norberg Chulz Ch. 1974 Meaning in Western Architecture, London.
Norberg Schulz Ch. 1984 Genius Loci, towards a phenomenology of architecture, New York
Orlandos A. 1958 Monastery Architecture, text and drawings, Athens, (Greek version).
Paléologue A. 1997 Le Mont Athos, merveille du christianisme byzantain,
Pallas D., 1965, "The Aesthetic Ideas of the Byzantines before the Conquest", ΕΕΒΣ 34
Pallasmaa J. 1993 *«Architecture in the making. An architecture of imaginery: conception and experience in Alvar Aalto's architecture».* Companion to contemporary architectural thought. London-New York
Papachrysanthou D. 1992 Athonite Monasticism, principles and organization, Athens, (Greek version)
Papagiannis T. & Father Eliseos Simonopetritis, 1994 Natural Space and Monasticism, the conservation of the Byzantine tradition in the Agion Oros, Athens, (Greek version)

Papadopoulos S. 1970 Analekta Blatadon 4 *"Meeting Orthodox and Scholastic Theology"* (Kallistou Aggelikoudi and Thomas Aquinas), Thessaloniki (Greek version),
Papaioannou Konstantinos Sp., 1977 The Greek Monasteries as architectural compositions, PhD, Faculty of Architecture, Metsovio National Polytechnic School Athens, Athens, (Greek version).
Papadopulos St. 1990 Patrology, Volume 2, IV Century (Eastern and Western (Greek version).
Papanoutsos E. P. 1971 Logos and Anthropos, Athens, (Greek version)
Papoutsopoulos H.N. 1980 Blaise Pascal, Athens, (Greek versión)
Pascal B. (19..) Thoughts, Athens.
Plotinus 1956-63, Enneades, E. Brehier (coll. des Universites de France), Societe de edition Les Belles Artes - Paris
Porphyrios D. 1982 Source of modern eclecticism, London
Prokopiou G., 1981 Secular Symbolism in the Byzantine Ecclesiastic Architecture, PhD, Faculty of Architecture, Metsovio National Polytechnic School Athens, Athens, (Greek version).
Saalman H.1962 Medieval Architecture General editor G.R. Collins Columbia University, New York.
Schildt G. 1986 Alvar Aalto, the decisive years. Rizzoli - New York
Scully V. 1961 Modern Architecture, The architecture of democracy, New York
Scully V. 1962 Louis I. Kahn, New York
Scully V. 1962 The earth, the temple and the Gods. Yale Univ. Press - New Haven and London
Scully V. 1965 Frank Lloyd Wright, New York
Sergeant J. 1976 Frank Lloyd Wright's Usonian Houses the case for organic architecture, New York
Serr J. 1979 La Filocalia de la oracion de Jesus. (Traducción realizada por el equipo de editiorial Lumen sobre

textos de la Patrologia Griega de Migne) Buenos Aires
Sherrard Ph. 1994 The Sacred in the life and in the art, Nea Smyrni, (Greek version).

Simeoforidis G. 1987 Le Corbusier, text for Greece, photos and drawings, Athens. (Greek version).
Siotou Markou, 1994 History and Theology of Holy Images, Athens, (Greek version)
Sitte C. 1965 City planning according to artistic principles, London.
Steppan T. 1995 Die Athos -Lavra, und der trikonchale kuppelnaos in der byzantinischen architektur. Ed. Maris - Müchen
Tachiaos A. E.1987/31 *«Hesychasm as a creative force in the fields of Arts and Literature»* L'art de Thessalonique et des pays Balkaniques et les Courants Spirituels au XIVe Siecle. Academie Serbe des sciences et des Arts / Institut des Etudes Balkaniques. Belgrado
Talbot Rice D. 1964 The Byzantines, London.
Tatakis V. 1977 The Byzantine Philosophy, Athens, (Greek version)
Theoharidis P. 3/1991 The architecture heritage of Agion Oros. Paratiritis, Thessaloniki, (Greek version)
Thomas D'Aquin 1984 Somme Theologique Tome 3 Les editions du Cerf - Paris
Velenis G. 1986 *"Historical Points of Change of Post Byzantine Architecture in Thessaloniki"*, Thessaloniki 2300 of Post Byzantine period 1430/1912, Thessaloniki, (Greek version).
Venturi R. 1977 Complexity and Contradiction in architecture. The museum of modern art. New York in assoc. with the Graham Foundation for advanced studies in the fine arts, Chicago New York
Velenis G. 1985 "The framework of laws influencing the development of the character of dwellings during

the Turkish occupation", Storia della Città 31-32, Milano, p. 33-36
Waisman M. 1980 Contextualismo *«Los multiples rostros del contextualismo»* Coleccion Summarios 57, Buenos Aires
Wright F. Ll. 1943 An autobiography, New York
Wright F. Ll. 1957 A testament, New York
Wright F. Ll. 1968 The early work, New York
Wright F. Ll. 1970 An organic architecture, the architecture of democracy (the Sir G. Watson Lectures of the Sulgrave manor board for 1939) The MIT press Cambridge -Massachusetts
Wright F. Ll. 1970 The Natural House, New York
Zafiropoulos S. 1998 *"Three Dances in the space"*, Orion, Honorary Volume D. Fatouro, p.207-215, Polytechnic School Aristotle University of Thessaloniki, Thessloniki, (Greek version)
Zevi B. 1973 Spazi dell'architettura Moderna. Giulio Einaudi ed. - Torino
Zizioulas I.1992 The Creation as Eucharistic, Theologise approach on the problem of ecology, Nea Smyrni, (Greek version)

Index

Prologue 5

Chapter 1
Ideas and Principles of Monastic Architecture 15

Chapter 2
Morphology of Monasteries and Nature 79

Chapter 3
Modern Architectural Thought as a Means to
Approach and Interpret Monastery Architecture 129

Chapter 4
Monastery Architecture and Residential Organization 151

Chapter 5
The Monastery and its Symbolism 175

Conclusion 199

Bibliography 205

www.ingramcontent.com/pod-product-compliance
Lightning Source LLC
Chambersburg PA
CBHW062209080426
42734CB00010B/1852